The Jim Carrey Scrapbook

The JIM CARREY

Scrapbook

Edited by

Scott and Barbara Siegel

A CITADEL PRESS BOOK
Published by Carol Publishing Group

A Citadel Press Book
Published by Carol Publishing Group
Citadel Press is a registered trademark of Carol Communications, Inc.
Editorial Offices: 600 Madison Avenue, New York, N.Y. 10022
Sales and Distribution Offices: 120 Enterprise Avenue, Secaucus, N.J. 07094
In Canada: Canadian Manda Group, One Atlantic Avenue, Suite 105, Toronto,
    Ontario M6K 3E7

Queries regarding rights and permissions should be addressed to Carol Publishing
Group, 600 Madison Avenue, New York, N.Y. 10022

Carol Publishing Group books are available at special discounts for bulk purchases,
sales promotion, fund-raising, or educational purposes. Special editions can be created to specifications. For details, contact: Special Sales Department, Carol Publishing
Group, 120 Enterprise Avenue, Secaucus, N.J. 07094

Manufactured in the United States of America
10 9 8 7 6 5 4 3 2 1

Library of Congress Cataloging-in-Publication Data

Siegel, Scott.
    The Jim Carrey scrapbook / edited by Scott and Barbara Siegel.
        p.   cm.
    "A Citadel Press book."
    ISBN 0-8065-1706-9 (pbk.)
    1. Carrey, Jim, 1962-   —Miscellanea. I. Siegel, Barbara.
II. Title.
PN 2287.C278S54   1995
791.43'028'092—dc20   95-19771
                                                              CIP

For David Nancoff——

There are very few genuinely unique people in the world, but David is
one of them. He's smart, creative, generous (to a fault), and keenly interested
in everyone and everything around him. Mostly, though, he's just the warmest,
funniest, most likable guy in North America. And that's despite the fact
that his all-time favorite movie is *Tokyo Decadence*. Then, again, maybe it's
because of it.

Acknowledgments

First and foremost we thank our publisher, Steven Schragis, who bought this book on a phone conversation, without seeing so much as a single sentence on paper. Thank you for your confidence and trust. We also offer our deep appreciation to our editor, Marcy Swingle, who was supportive and "there" for us at every turn. Among those who helped us in our photo research, we happily thank our dear friend Jami Bernard as well as the folks at New Line, Morgan Creek, Warner Bros., Movie Star News, Photofest, and Globe Photos.

INTRODUCTION

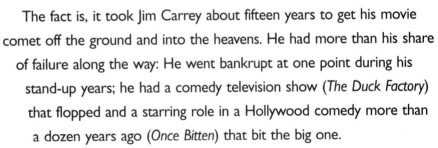

There isn't a performer on this planet who is hotter right now than Jim Carrey. From *Ace Ventura: Pet Detective* to *Batman Forever* and beyond, Jim Carrey is doing more than smokin'; he's burnin'! He appeared to be an overnight sensation, a blazing comedy comet, who suddenly blazed his way across the celluloid sky. And it's true. Sort of.

The fact is, it took Jim Carrey about fifteen years to get his movie comet off the ground and into the heavens. He had more than his share of failure along the way: He went bankrupt at one point during his stand-up years; he had a comedy television show (*The Duck Factory*) that flopped and a starring role in a Hollywood comedy more than a dozen years ago (*Once Bitten*) that bit the big one.

Jim Carrey, however, gets the last laugh, and we've had the opportunity to laugh along with him in *Ace Ventura: Pet Detective*, *The Mask*, *Dumb and Dumber*, and *Batman Forever*, each one a bigger hit than the one before. Now comes *Ace Ventura: When Nature Calls*, and his fans—and we count ourselves among them—can't wait to start laughing again. And we know the laughter will continue long after his latest film, because he's already committed to making *The Mask II*. After that comes *Cable Guy* and *Liar, Liar,* comedies he signed to make for a record-making $20 million each.

And why not pay him that kind of cash? After all, there isn't a single star in Hollywood who has Jim Carrey's incredible track record: four movies in a row that have earned over $100 million. Stallone can't match that. Schwarzenegger can't match that. Costner can't match that. Nobody can even touch it. Talk about laughing all the way to the bank! The money he's making, though, is just a side issue. The side-splitting comedy he's creating is the real treasure. In ort, Jim Carrey is always inventive, always surprising, always outrageous. He is, without doubt, the comic phenomenon of the 1990s.

Our own introduction to Jim Carrey came when the lights dimmed in the Warner Bros. screening room in New York and *Ace Ventura: Pet Detective* began to play. We had no idea who the star of the movie was. We had heard something about his being "the white guy on *In Living Color*." We had never seen the show, so Jim Carrey was just a name to us. Within the first five minutes of the movie, though, we looked at each other and simultaneously said, "He's Jerry Lewis!" And that was a compli-

ment. We were hooked—on the film and on Jim Carrey. The guy was incredible; he was even acting with his teeth! Since then, we've followed Jim Carrey's career with ever-increasing delight and respect.

By the time *Dumb and Dumber* was released, we knew we wanted to write something about him, but a conventional biography seemed like a rather stale approach to someone so visually electric. Besides, there's no way to capture his comic sensibility by merely recounting the events of his life. That's when the idea of doing *The Jim Carrey Scrapbook* occurred to us.

Unlike a regular biography, this book is intended to be all things to all people who love Jim Carrey. If you want to learn more about Jim Carrey's life, the *Scrapbook* provides his biography in entertaining detail. If it's the movies that you love, well, just take a look at the nearly one hundred photos! And if it's Jim Carrey's unique sense of humor that has drawn you to this book,

Jim did something no other movie star has ever done: made four $100 million grossing movies in a row: *Ace Ventura: Pet Detective, The Mask, Dumb and Dumber,* and *Batman Forever*. And he did it without repeating himself. Each of his four characters is largely different from the other, with the emphasis on large (as in ego).

you will not be disappointed, because first and foremost, *The Jim Carrey Scrapbook* was conceived, written, and designed to be in the Jim Carrey comic mode. The humor you will find in this book is not recycled Jim Carrey jokes; rather, it is comedy inspired by Jim Carrey. Or, if you will, it is a reflection and a celebration of Jim Carrey's gloriously dumb humor.

This book includes the sort of stuff you will not find in any other scrapbook. Feeling like a brain surgeon? Well, open up Jim Carrey's brain and take a look at how it works. Or consider what television would be like if Jim Carrey had his own network. Then there's the Jim Carrey Body-Parts Jigsaw Puzzle. And what about all those old movies Jim might someday remake? Consider also all those lists, tests, quizzes, and puzzles to separate the dumb from the dumber.

Yes, it's all here. Well, not actually here. You have to turn some pages.

JIM CARREY'S COMIC FAMILY TREE

His mother, Jerrilina, had a major influence on young Jim. Among other things, Jerrilina's son now has a deep and abiding fear of fruit.

Jim's father, Jerry, was so happy at the birth of his son that he couldn't see straight. Moments later, however, he tried to kill the kid with a straight razor.

Surrounded by his "relatives," perhaps you can see the family resemblance?

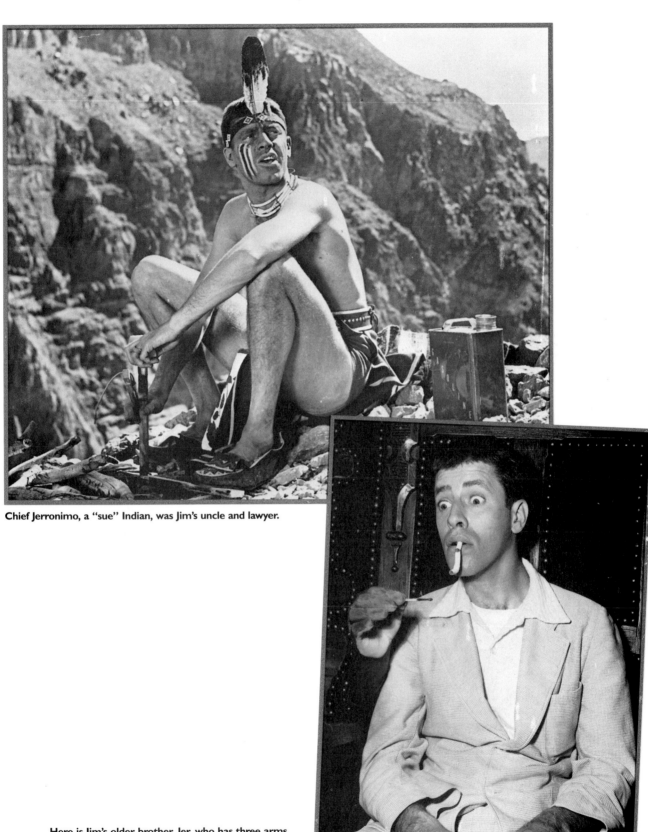

Chief Jerronimo, a "sue" Indian, was Jim's uncle and lawyer.

Here is Jim's older brother, Jer, who has three arms.
It's a sad story that we'd rather not get into.

See, we told you there were a lot of pictures.

"The White Guy" on *In Living Color*; Carrey's talent would eventually spread to Hollywood feature films.

The Jim Carrey Scrapbook

The

JIM CARREY

STORY

The young Jim Carrey would sit for hours and hours in front of a mirror, twisting and torturing his face, memorizing the muscles that would transform him into a lipless ghoul or, in an instant, a startling replica of James Dean until he could do it without looking in the mirror. Then came the test: He would turn to his family and friends, making them collapse in laughter as his vulcanized face and frame contorted itself into impossibly funny postures and expressions.

Now he does the same thing in front of tens of millions of people all over the world. And he gets the same results. At this point in his career, Jim Carrey has reached the rare and rarefied strata that all actors seek and few achieve; the

Nothing cautious about Carrey here. He's letting it all hang out at the twentieth birthday celebration of The Comedy Store.

The pictures are so amazing that we figured it was worth a second look. Carrey is seen with Richard Belzer (reaching for the sock), Bob Saget, and Pauly Shore.

ability to draw people to a movie theater on the basis of his name alone.

But where did Jim Carrey come from? Who is he? What is he like? What is the source of his humor?

Well, in person, Carrey isn't "Jim Carrey" all the time. Tall, impishly handsome, with a good-looking cap over the chipped-tooth smile he flashed for real in *Dumb and Dumber*, he certainly possesses the potential to run amok at a moment's notice—to suddenly start speaking in comic tongues, channeling ridiculous beings from the vapors, contorting his body.

Except he doesn't do it. "It would be awfully sick to wake up and think that as soon as I leave my room I've got to be that guy," he says. "I think people would be disappointed when they met me if I was jumping around like an idiot. There's nothing more embarrassing than somebody who's on all the time."

Yet he's tempted. He can sometimes barely contain himself. Some of it is inherent; he was born with a talent. But what drives him is something else entirely. The intensity Carrey brings to crafting his comedy reflects the years of pain, disappointment, and frustration—of knowing he was capable of making millions

Here's Jim trying to be "nice and normal."

Underneath that "nice and normal" visage, however, is a "raging beast."

JIM CARREY'S BRAIN: A User's Manual and Map of the Stars' Homes

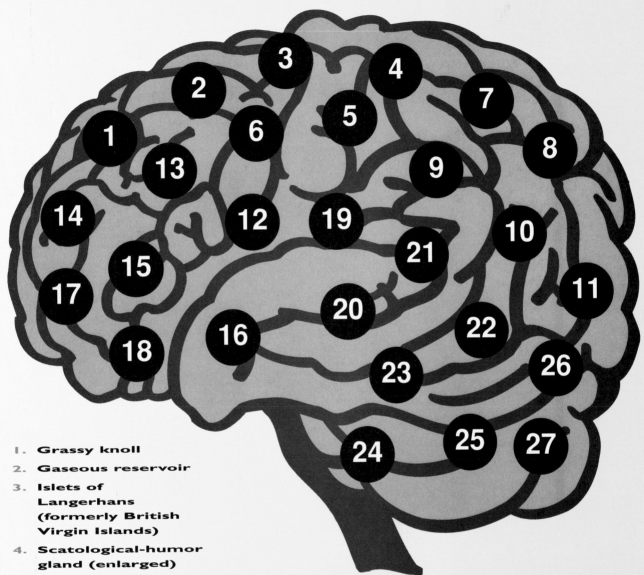

1. **Grassy knoll**
2. **Gaseous reservoir**
3. **Islets of Langerhans (formerly British Virgin Islands)**
4. **Scatological-humor gland (enlarged)**
5. **Animal hair**
6. **Area of lost marbles**
7. **Cerebellum of St. Mary's**
8. **Ego**
9. **Id**
10. **Superego**
11. **Super-duper ego**
12. **Really swell ego**
13. **Sebaceous cyst (repeat rapidly twelve times)**
14. **Book depository**
15. **Second gunman**
16. **Seat of reason**
17. **Chaise longue of unreason**
18. **Laz-ee Boy recliner of antireason**
19. **EEG**
20. **KGB**
21. **Jim Nabor's ranch**
22. **Spare tire**
23. **Spare brain (inflatable)**
24. **Spare brain pump**
25. **First-aid Kit**
26. **Funny bone**
27. **Soup bone**

JIM CARREY'S TOP-TEN FAVORITE FOODS

1. Puppy Chow pizza

2. Burger-in-a-bottle

3. Bread balls and gum

4. Wiener juice

5. Gummy Fries

6. Pork-Chop-Chip Ice Cream

7. Hamsicles

8. Ketchup cake

9. Pickle-nut cookies

10. Liver loaf

laugh but of not getting the chance. The humor cuts close to the edge because that's how Carrey likes to live; he spent too much time on the other side, wishing for a chance to show what he could do to allow himself to be cautious now. And the comedy is a vent, a valve to let off steam from a lifetime of bad breaks and humiliations no kid should have to go through. There were painful family experiences that gave Carrey the resolve to do what he most loved and succeed at it. They were also dark memories to feed the fire to get it done.

Because as nice and normal as Carrey appears when you talk to him, there is a raging beast inside, still embarrassed and upset about the demeaning experiences of his youth. As he once told *Playboy*, "My focus is to forget the pain of life. Forget the pain, mock the pain, reduce it. And laugh."

Born January 17, 1962, in Newmarket, Ontario, Canada, near Toronto, Carrey was the youngest of four children. They moved to nearby Aurora when Jim was a toddler and stayed there until his eighth year.

Dubbed "Jimmy Gene the string bean," he was hung with the middle name Eugene: "I figured my parents called me that to keep me humble," he told *People* magazine. "You can never get too cool with a name like Eugene."

He was a thin, happy kid, one who gave his parents fits because he didn't like to eat.

But the skinny child would sit back and refuse—and then, when he had everyone's attention, he would work the room, making faces until adults and siblings alike were roaring with laughter.

The shows at home continued; anytime company was over, the family invariably said, "Look what Jim can do," and the show began. He'd do impressions of the neighbors, his own family, people he saw on television, and the appreciative basement crowd would howl with laughter.

"I got a lot of support from my parents," he told Barbara Walters in March 1995. "They didn't tell me I was being stupid. They said I was being funny."

"I've always been gangly—spastic is the word, I think," he told the *Fort Worth Star-Telegram*. "I've just basically harnessed spasticness. You'd think I'd be incredible at sports and stuff. I was a good hockey player growing up in Canada, but track and field, I was hopeless."

He would spend hours at a time making up and acting out little shows in front of the mirror, trying on faces and voices, and having conversations with himself.

"It was so much fun to sit in my room and talk to myself in different voices," he told Walters. "My mother told me to stop because if I looked too long, I would see the devil. That was the worst thing she could have said. It made me look more. I thought maybe he and I could make a deal."

What's the key to making a funny face?

THE JIM CARREY EDITION
of the Very Special Olympics

All eyes are on Saskatoon, Canada, where amateur-class clowns from around the world are gathering for the first Jim Carrey Olympiad. Record crowds have come to this picturesque village's new Olympic-size bowling alley, where they wait the ceremonial passing of Olympic gas. The world holds its nose.

Highlights of this year's events include:

SLIPPED-DISCUS RACE

Long hours of training could pay off as double-jointed geeks from fifteen nations duck-walk, lurch, careen, mince, twitch, and teeter toward the finish line.

SHATNER SOUND-OFF

Not for the squeamish. For two hours, three-men teams will impersonate William Shatner as Captain James T. Kirk, repeatedly barking, "Spock!" with exaggerated, clipped delivery.

CAREER-PITFALL POLE VAULT

Armed with copies of John Travolta's resumé, contestants must clear hurdles that include the Eddie Murphy Bad Script Cesspool, the Chevy Chase Pit of Doom, and the harrowing Jerry Lewis Grease Slick.

SCATOLOGICAL THROW

Contestants will "scat" freestyle after completing a required succession of bodily-function noises and physical sight gags, including flatulence, belching and heartburn, extreme nasal drip, and difficult BMs.

GRECO-ROMAN GRIMACING, INDIVIDUAL

Rubber-faced participants will execute facial tics, mugging, and exaggerated eye rolls. Finalists will continue with the extremely dangerous mandible throw, attempting the elusive open-mouth, ear-to-ear grins that stop just short of actual jaw dislocation.

All righty, then! Let the games begin!

"It's an inner weirdness," Jim said. "It's not so much the face—anybody can do something with their face—but it's the insanity that bubbles beneath the surface that comes through."

"It's an inner weirdness," he told the *Chicago Tribune*. "It's not so much the face—anybody can do something with their face—but it's the insanity that bubbles beneath the surface that comes through."

Still, he was quiet and shy at school until the family moved to Toronto. Then, one day on the playground, he began testing funny lines on his new acquaintances, showing them a few of his impressions, and bang-o! Suddenly he was popular.

"For some reason I did something where I realized I could get a reaction," he told *Saturday Night* magazine. "That was when I broke out of my shell at school, because I really didn't have any friends or anything like that and I just kind of was going along, and then finally I did this zany thing, and all of a sudden I had tons of friends."

He was an A student, one who finished his work quickly and then began putting on little shows for a select audience in the immediate vicinity of his desk. "I was like a ninja class clown," he told the *Chicago Tribune* of his sneak-attack comedy, performed whenever the teacher's back was turned.

The teacher inevitably grew weary of the constant waves of suppressed giggles from Carrey's audience and finally said one day, "If you think you're so funny, Mr. Carrey, why don't you come up to the front of the class and try it from here?"

This might be considered Carrey's first open-mike experience—except that most fledgling comedians don't have an appreciative audience of nine-year-olds waiting to explode at impressions of the Three Stooges and the school principal.

Before long, one wise teacher figured out the way to utilize the excess comic steam Carrey built up doing classwork.

JIM CARREY'S TOP-TEN DREAM OLYMPIC EVENTS

1. **2-meter dash**

2. **Hop, skip, and spit**

3. **Discus drop**

4. **Javelin coloring**

5. **Hurdle lifting**

6. **Synchronized nose-picking**

7. **Shotput roll**

8. **10-meter back float**

9. **Compulsory belly flop with twist**

10. **Official torch dropper**

Wonder if any of Jim's teachers ever imagined his entertaining classmates in just this fashion?

Like Stanley Ipkiss in *The Mask*, Jim was a shy young fellow.

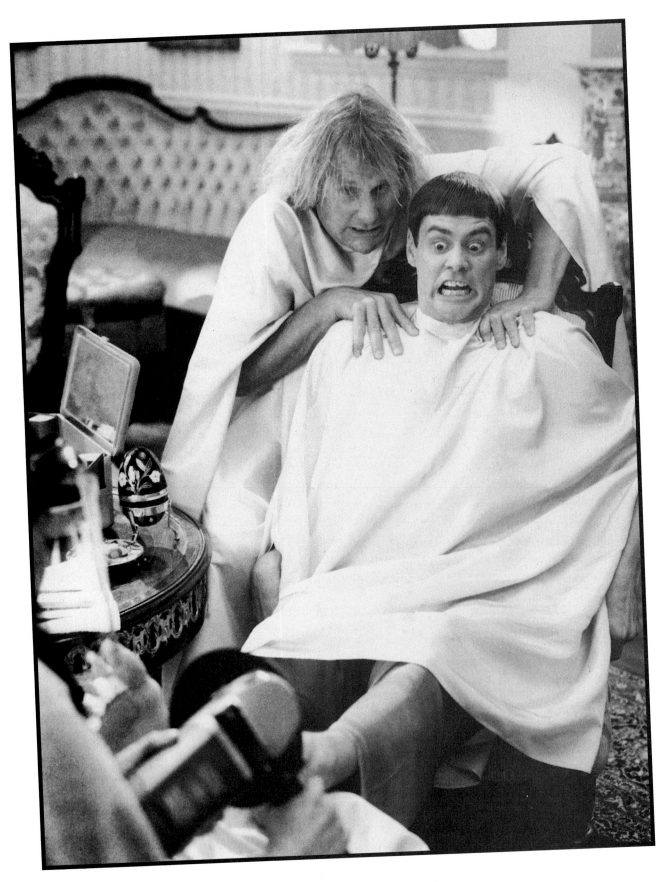

This is as close as Lloyd Christmas (Jim Carrey) gets to an orgasm in *Dumb and Dumber*. **Jeff Daniels looks on with stupefied concern.**

"I had this one teacher who gave me fifteen minutes at the end of each class to do a routine," Carrey told the *Fort Worth Star-Telegram*, "with the personal guarantee that I wouldn't disrupt the class the rest of the time. So I'd sit there and finish my work, then start working on my set."

What kind of material? "I'd chew up a pack of heart-shaped powdered candies," he told *Time* magazine, "then act like I was sick and throw up every color of the rainbow. For no reason, just that I could do it."

But there was a method to this madness: Carrey loved movies and television comedians and from a young age dreamed of being one himself. At the age of ten, in fact, he sent his resumé, such as it was, to Carol Burnett.

"I was lucky I always knew what I wanted," he told *Parade* magazine. He told *Playboy*, "I can't imagine what it's like not to know what you want to do. People come out of college not knowing. It's weird. I can't imagine that. It must be a horrible feeling. I knew what I wanted from the time I was a little kid."

Why? The payoff, of course: those big hearty peals of laughter that are the reward—the lifeblood—of the successful comedian.

"If you had the urge and nobody laughed, it'd be really horrifying," he told the *Detroit News*. "But when you realize you can do it, you can really make somebody laugh, it's not a power thing. It's just a great feeling. It's like giving somebody an orgasm.

"It's like if you have good sex and you know you've made the other person happy, it's so much better than doing it for yourself. Although if you're using your left hand, it's really like you're with someone else."

George Carlin, Steve Martin, and Cheech and Chong were the prevalent comedy voices of the day, but Carrey found himself drawn elsewhere: the physical humor of Jerry Lewis, Peter Sellers, and Dick Van Dyke and the upright goodness of James Stewart.

"If you want to know my kind of hero, it's Jimmy Stewart in *Mr. Smith Goes to Washington*, he told the *Detroit News*. "It's somebody who gives the regular Joe out there hope that he can take on a Goliath."

Van Dyke, however, was a key inspiration.

"I still watch the old show and just howl," Carrey told the *Fort Worth Star-Telegram*. "He had it all going on, you know. He had the physical funniness—I don't think any joke can make me laugh like some physical thing. There's something about that."

Carrey got an example at home from his father, Percy, a onetime jazz musician who, as Carrey always claims, was the funniest member of the family.

"My father was nuts," he told the *Detroit News*. "He was the type of guy that if you met him for five minutes, you'd feel like you'd known him for fifty years: open, crazy, always looking for the laugh. The guy that puts a stocking on his head and runs up in front of your car when you're coming in the driveway, that's him."

Percy kept the family laughing and happy even when money was tight, even though his own dreams had been quashed.

JIM CARREY'S TOP-TEN FAVORITE JOBS

1. Pickle sorter
2. Dog-toy tester
3. Twist-tie inspector
4. U.S. government monkey counter
5. Lint removist
6. Cat nanny
7. Doughnut courier
8. Trainee, Toothpick World
9. Mustard Boy–Burger Doodle
10. Toenail model

"He was a sax and clarinet player—it was like a Hollywood script," Carrey told *Playboy*. "He sold his sax to get my sister out of the hospital when she was born. And he never went back to music."

Then, as Carrey was entering teenhood—at the age at which seeming cool is the most important thing in life—the unthinkable happened. Percy, who had been controller for a company for twenty-five years, was laid off at the age of fifty-one and was unable to find work as an accountant.

He took the only work he could get—as a janitor at the Titan Wheel factory. Before long, everyone in the family was working there as well, showing up after school to suit up and sweep floors and clean rest rooms.

"I'm not as nice as my dad," Jim said. Look at that face and you can believe it.

"I spent eight hours after school scraping pubic hair off urinals," Carrey told Barbara Walters.

The effect was devastating: Aside from the fact that Carrey was falling asleep in school because he was working a full-time job, his family lost their house. They moved into a Volkswagon van and, later, into a tent in the backyard of a relative's house.

"At a certain point, everything just went south," he says. "I got a serious edge from that experience."

Wayne Flemming, a stand-up comic, and friend from Toronto, recalled for Knight-Ridder newspapers the night he gave Carrey a ride home from a comedy club. Carrey motioned the car over and got out next to a van parked at the curb. Flemming asked Carrey, "what's this?"

In his first attempt at stand-up comedy, Jim was dressed in a yellow polyester suit. It didn't work out for him then, but it sure worked for him—at least the yellow part—in *The Mask*.

"This is where we all sleep," Carrey told him.

As Carrey told *Newsweek*. "I slept in class because I was working in the factory for eight hours after school. I've gone through periods where I look at street guys and I know that's me. I know how they got there."

He told *Playboy*: "It made me mad. Seeing my dad do that kind of work just tore me up. And it made me realize that there's no such thing as security. It provided me with motivation: Since nothing is secure, I should go after what I love."

Still, he told *Parade* magazine, "We had problems like all families, but we had a lot of love. I was extremely loved. We always felt we had each other."

Carrey had to help keep his family afloat. He dropped out of school, living a Dickensian childhood of full-time, soul-killing work while existing in a tent with a half-dozen other people.

"We were incredibly unhappy, and we were turning into monsters, racists—things that we weren't," he told *Parade*. "It was a learning experience. I understood why people who put themselves in a wrong situation in life can really lose their soul and spirit. I didn't have any friends because I didn't want them.

Carrey was growing up fast. "When I turned fifteen," he told *Rolling Stone*, "I said to myself, 'I'm not going to reach sixteen without losing my virginity.'" At a party, he "got totally fried" and went upstairs with a woman ten years his senior. He remembered that Styx's *Grand Illusion* was playing while they did the deed. After that night he never saw the woman again.

He quit school when he turned sixteen. "I was working eight hours a day," he told *Parade* magazine, "and I just didn't understand the teacher anymore."

Miserable day and night, young Jim fought the pain with comedy.

"My grandparents were alcoholics and my grandfather would get my dad in a corner every Christmas and tell him what a loser he was because he didn't have a job," Carrey recalled for *Parade*. "My father would just sit there and turn purple with anger. It was horrible for me to watch because he was such a nice man. But I'm not as nice as my dad. As soon as my grandparents would leave, I'd imitate them. My father would be so relieved, it was as if I pulled the pressure plug when I went into this routine."

But the effects of trying to beat poverty finally got to the Carrey clan, he told *Parade*: "After nearly two years of living like this, we finally said, 'This just isn't us. We don't like people anymore.' So we quit our jobs and chose poverty. We got a VW camper and went

Five Things
Jim Carrey Can't Do

1. **BE NAMED POPE**

   Naturally, the College of Cardinals approached Jim, but he has his own strict code of conduct. When Jim wears a long brocade dress, he insists on the correct makeup, elbow-length gloves, and stiletto heels.

2. **CLEAN UP THE MESS IN WASHINGTON, D.C.**

   Oh, sure, he could—if he had enough plutonium. Anybody could clean up Washington if they had enough plutonium.

3. **SLEEP WITH SHARON STONE**

   When Sharon comes for a sleepover, nobody gets any snooze.

4. **TALK JEFF DANIELS INTO DOING HIS OWN STUNTS**

   Not after that scene where he puts his tongue on the frost. Jeff isn't usually one to hold a grudge, but he was actually overheard saying angrily, "At od amn Im Arrey, ah'll et im if it's a ast ing ah ooo."

5. **TOUCH HIS NOSE TO HIS ELBOW**

   Actually, he can, but he's not allowed to reveal his method. (The Union of Double-Jointed Comedians forbids the telling of its secrets.)

camping for eight months. One by one we got jobs and then moved back into a house."

At the age of fifteen, Carrey also took one particularly momentous step: He stood onstage at a comedy club for the first time. Knowing his son was dying to try it, Percy took the initiative and booked Jim a slot at Yuk Yuk's, one of Toronto's first comedy clubs. Then he drove him to the gig—and total disaster followed.

"I got booed off the stage," he told *Playboy*. "I was dressed in a yellow polyester suit that my mom told me would be a good idea. She said all the young men were wearing them—she'd seen it on *Donahue.*"

Carrey was carrying a ventriloquist's dummy and doing impressions—none of which the audience responded to. As if his clothes weren't bad enough, Carrey had to contend with the club's owner, who stood in the wings heckling him on an open mike.

Jim learned to mimic just about everyone, although he hardly looks like Roy Rogers in this picture. More like Dale Evans, don't you think?

"He would be back there saying, 'Totally boring—totally boring,' and playing excerpts from *Jesus Christ Superstar*, the part where they're singing, 'Crucify him! Crucify him!' " Carrey told Barbara Walters. According to an account in *Saturday Night* magazine, the club manager ended the act by yelling, "Enough! Enough! Get off the stage!"

It took Carrey two years to get up the nerve to try again. "I have no idea what motivated me to try again," he told *Parade*. "I just felt like giving it a shot. Failure taught me that failure isn't the end unless you give up."

This time, minus the yellow suit, he was a hit. He became one of the sensations of Toronto, working steadily and amassing a local following with a polished act of comedy impressions. He could do anyone, it seemed, particularly under pressure: from Bruce Dern to Cher, from James Dean to Clint Eastwood.

Jim Carrey on the stand-up circuit.

In February 1981 he received the kind of review from the *Toronto Star* that performers dream of: "I saw a genuine star coming to life, and that happens so rarely that it's worth shouting out the news to the world," wrote Bruce Blackader. "Jim Carrey—here he comes." Watching Carrey, he wrote, "was probably like seeing Woody Allen for the first time in Greenwich Village. And I'm not kidding, folks. Jim Carrey is really that good."

With that as his calling card, Carrey headed for Los Angeles at the age of seventeen. He arrived and checked into a low-rent hotel in one of the seedier sections of Sunset Strip.

"There were hookers all over the place, which I'd never seen in my life," Carrey told *USA Today*. "They were coming up asking me for dates, and I thought it

was Sadie Hawkins Day. It was really like stepping into a Scorsese movie to me. It was like, 'Where am I? Who am I?' The town felt so big."

Or, as he told the *New York Times*, "It was like a complete other world. It was like I had walked into some bizarre X-rated movie. It freaked me out."

This first trip to Los Angeles, just like his first attempt at stand-up, was a washout. He flopped and headed back home to Toronto to lick his wounds and continue honing his skills. Two years later, now nineteen years old and armed with a better idea of what to expect in Los Angeles, he began to make a name for himself at the Comedy Store, then the center of the comedians' world in Los Angeles. Soon he became the hottest impressionist working the comedy circuit because of his rubberized

Jim was "on the road to Vegas," but he decided to take a detour. He's seen here with costar Jeff Daniels from *Dumb and Dumber.*

As a stand-up comic, Jim created all of his own material. And this time, he apparently liked what he wrote.

face and seemingly inexhaustible supply of characters. From Gandhi surreptitiously eating potato salad during a hunger strike to a mutated Elvis with little flipper arms, Carrey's was the act to catch if you were in the know. He was so confident a performer that he would even take requests, improvising entire routines while imitating the famous name that had been suggested only moments before.

He was suddenly in demand in Las Vegas, opening for, or going on the road with, Rodney Dangerfield, the Pointer Sisters, Sheena Easton, Pat Boone, and Andy Williams. He even did a television special with Rich Little.

Everything happened very quickly. Before he knew it, he was making more than $200,000 a year. He paid for his parents to move to Los Angeles and into his house, then began supporting them with performing fees that were growing steadily.

At the same time, however, he felt as if he were slowly going out of his mind. He was unhappy personally and professionally and felt it was time for a change.

So he scrapped his entire act—gave up being an impressionist for what could instead be called comic impressionism: wild, stream-of-consciousness riffs that took him deep into his own psyche and out to the comic beyond.

As he said to *Parade*, "I knew I could end up making a million dollars a year, but I didn't care. I wanted to create for myself. An impressionist never gets to be himself." And he told *Newsweek*, "I was down the road to Vegas and I didn't want to go there."

"I was putting out something that I didn't want to become known for," he told *Saturday Night* magazine. "I wanted to be myself, to create some things that had never been done before, rather than constantly sitting waiting for the next famous person whom I could impersonate. That held nothing for me. It was a slow realization but at one point I just said, 'Never again.'

"Everybody was saying, 'Oh man, don't do that, you're looking a gift horse in the mouth. It will all go away.' I knew in my heart that I could do it, but the only way to prove that I could do it was to just cut it off completely for a while. I just figured, if I cut my right arm off, sooner or later I'll learn to write with my left hand.'"

Jim's parents might have reacted badly to the news that he could no longer support them, but they didn't. Happily, though, Jim had an Ace up his sleeve.

BLAME IT ON JIM

Too modest to take credit for the breathtaking scope of his accomplishments, Jim has been quietly involved in a wide array of activities over the years—often with history-making results. Here, for the first time, meet:

JIM CARREY, POLITICAL ADVISER

Jim has been a friend of Bill's for years. He introduced the young Governor Clinton to an ardent supporter, Paula Jones. He gave investment advice: Buy Whitewater. He loaned Bill his barber for that famous haircut and suggested health care as the issue to make his mark as a new president.

JIM CARREY GRANT, LADIES' MAN

When Jim introduced Beatle John Lennon to Yoko Ono, it upset another friend. Jim evened the score by helping Paul McCartney pick up Linda Eastman.

GYM CARREY, ATHLETIC SUPPORTER

As go-between for the players and the owners, Jim was kept hopping. Would the baseball strike have lasted as long as it did without his help? Who knows.

LORD JIM CARREY, ADVISER TO THE BRITISH THRONE

When Queen Elizabeth II wanted to update the monarchy's stodgy image, she turned to Jim. He suggested that Charles marry someone fresh and young and photogenic.

JIM CARREY, HUMANITARIAN

Where will he turn up next? Rumor has it that Jim is giving Newt Gingrich assertiveness training.

Thus started a two-year period in which Carrey dropped out of stand-up and took acting lessons, wrote poetry, started sculpting and painting.

Unfortunately, he had also invited his parents out to live with him: "I was trying to be Elvis: 'I bought you Graceland, Mama,'" he told Barbara Walters. "I was trying to be the good son, the lifesaver. I think I know what a nervous breakdown feels like."

He finally found himself going broke: "I had to tell them that they were on their own," he told *Parade*. "I wanted to save them, and I tried, but I finally ran out of money. They supported my decision, although it scared them."

His new material was darker, more personal, but also wilder and funnier. He became known as the comedian's comedian, with his gift for mimicry (he used impressions as seasoning rather than as the meat and potatoes of his act), his gangly body, and his double-jointed face.

"It's a trip into the dark and gloomy psyche of a lunatic," he told *Florida Today*, describing what his act became. "I talk a lot about behavioral stuff. Usually about the dark impulses you have to do strange things,

Jim Carrey takes up performance art.

Seen here with *Duck Factory* costar Julie Payne, Carrey seemed to be ready to knock on Hollywood's door, which happened to be right behind him.

Jim Carrey arrived for work in *The Duck Factory*, his new television series, with high hopes.

Carrey headed up a talented cast in *The Duck Factory*. His costars (clockwise) were Jay Tarses, Julie Payne, Teresa Ganzel, Jack Gilford, Don Messick, Clarence Gilyard Jr., and Nancy Lane. The show premiered on April 12, 1984, and disappeared thirteen weeks later.

like when you're on the seventh floor of a building and you see the pool and you figure, 'If I pushed off I could hit it.' The little weird thoughts you get. It's kind of like therapy for me, you know?"

As he told *Playboy*, "I started to do it for myself. Weird things. Don't try to please the crowd, shock them. If it's not funny, call it performance art. That's when everything started happening." When Carrey finally did find work with his new act, a club owner took one look at the strange material and demanded that Carrey replace it with his impressions. Carrey refused, telling the man to fire him if necessary. Impressed, the owner

let him go back on. The crowds responded, and the owner was contrite.

Carrey thought it all had finally paid off in 1984, when he was cast as the lead in *The Duck Factory*, an NBC sitcom that was being highly touted by the network. He was to play a naive comic strip artist from Minneapolis.

On all sides, Carrey was told that this was it: The match had been set to the fuse of the skyrocket that was his career.

"I had a big sitcom that was on between *Cheers* and *Hill Street Blues*, two of the hottest shows around—I was a made man," he says. "Then, after thirteen episodes, it disappeared.

Is Jim Carrey looking at Lauren Hutton's hand in this still from *Once Bitten*? Don't think so.

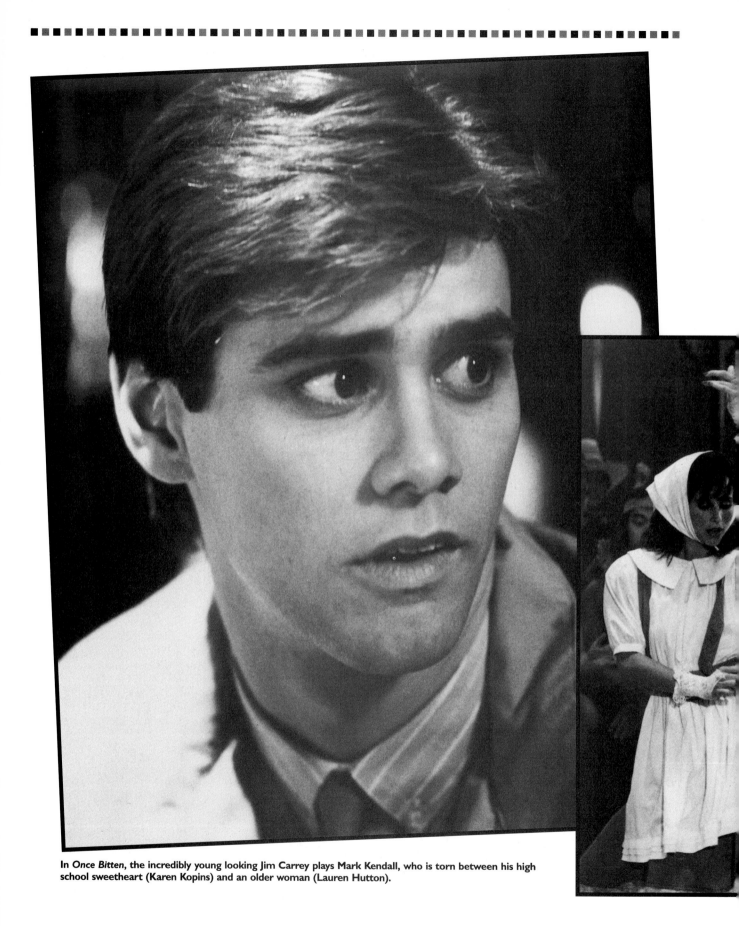

In *Once Bitten*, the incredibly young looking Jim Carrey plays Mark Kendall, who is torn between his high school sweetheart (Karen Kopins) and an older woman (Lauren Hutton).

"You go through the thing where you get an opportunity, where people are telling you, 'This is it.' Then it doesn't work out. And suddenly you start to hear, 'Well, he's had his shot.'

"But I never believed it. I always kind of believed in miracles. Some way, something was going to pop out."

Yet it didn't. Not for several years.

However, he did have a starring role in a movie that, like *The Duck Factory*, came and went in a flash. The film was *Once Bitten* (1985), a comic horror movie in which he played opposite the fetching Lauren Hutton. It wasn't a very good movie, but it's fascinating to watch as a curiosity piece; after all, he wouldn't star in a movie again for nearly a decade.

During the next several years, Carrey continued playing nightclubs, using the Comedy Store as his base. It was there that he met singer Linda Ronstadt, who was looking for a comedian to open her act. Instead, they became a couple, having a short, torrid affair.

Another romantic relationship came into being at the Comedy Store as well. Melissa Womer, an aspiring actress who waited tables there, befriended him. She had known him for two years, watching him go from big-time comedian to struggling performance artist, having recognized early on that he was someone and something special. After two years, they finally became a couple. They married on March 28, 1987.

Imagine what Jim Carrey would do on the dance floor in this scene from *Once Bitten* if he were making the same movie today? Karen Kopins is on Carrey's right; Lauren Hutton is on his left.

Carrey's ability at physical humor was more apparent in this playful offscreen moment with Lauren Hutton than it was in their movie together, *Once Bitten.*

The years they were dating, though, were marked by struggle. He began an inner journey, consulting psychics, psychologists, even colonic therapists. He would do his sets at the Comedy store (for twenty-five dollars a night), then head up into the hills overlooking Sunset Blvd. by himself in his car.

"For years I used to drive up to Mulholland Drive every night and look at the city and sit and imagine myself with all this money and being sought after," he told the *New York Times.* As he explained to Barbara Walters, "By the time I'd drive down, I had convinced myself that I *was* a big star, that all the best directors wanted to do projects with me. And I would feel much better."

He landed a few film parts—*Peggy Sue Got Married, The Dead Pool, Earth Girls Are Easy*—and the latter proved to be the key to his future. In the throwaway rock-and-roll comedy, he was one of three aliens from outer space who land in the San Fernando Valley and befriend a Valley girl and her circle of friends. One of the aliens was played by Jeff Goldblum, who was married

to the film's leading lady, Geena Davis. The other one was played by Damon Wayans, an old friend from the Comedy Store. The two of them all but stole the film with nearly silent performances marked by adept physical comedy. Jim's mastery of his body and his elastic face, in fact, would make him a prime candidate to be a mime, except for one thing: "I could never shut up long enough. I'd be going, 'I'm trapped in a box! Now I'm pulling a rope!' "

Carrey later told *Playboy* about the time Damon Wayans came backstage to see him after he did something particularly weird in his act. "He said, 'Hey, man, you are one of the angriest people that I have ever seen.' I said, 'Yeah, I guess I've got that going for me. That's how I deal with it.' There's an edge, a danger to what I do. And an anger. I do this ridiculous stuff that's based on anger and anxiety. Even the guys I play in the movies, nice guys, put their foot down. They're angry guys."

In 1990 his friendship with Damon Wayans paid off when Damon's brother, Keenen Ivory Wayans, began

Here's a young man with a future, although at this point in his life the success he yearned for must have seemed far away.

JIM CARREY'S DATING TIPS

Ask yourself: How could a slobby yutz like Jim Carrey get a delicious babe like Courteney Cox in Ace Ventura? Stumped? Wonder no more. Jim's secret savoir faire is now no secret. Guys, according to Jim himself, here's what works:

LOUD BEHAVIOR. Forget about women wanting a sensitive, caring guy. Women don't like wishy-washy wimps. They really want someone strong who takes charge. Insist on a hockey game for a first date. Try screaming high-pitched insults at the players and then point to your date when some murderous, pea-brained oaf climbs into the stands. If she makes it to dinner—preferably at a dirty bar with topless waitresses—bray orders and colorful comments at the top of your lungs. On the way home, don't forget to scream at the jerk ahead of you in traffic to get the lead out.

MASCULINE SCENT. It's pheromones that make her moan. Only idiots take showers and use cologne. Nothing reels in the fair sex faster than a good whiff of natural male odor. To enhance the effect, be sure to accentuate your wardrobe with items that have been lying in the laundry hamper for at least two months.

REGULAR-GUY STYLE. Don't try putting on airs around women. After all, you're no Cary Grant. But you can be Jim Carrey. Put her at ease with the kind of behavior she saw in her brothers growing up. Emitting gas at either end of your intestinal tract is fine, even encouraged. Drippy nose? That's what sleeves are for. And a good dirty joke lets her know you have a fine, down-home sense of humor.

MONEY. Some fool started the myth that women are impressed by guys with fat wallets. Bull. Women today are proud of their financial independence. So when the check comes for dinner, have her pay.

COMPLIMENTS. Nothing turns a gal's head faster than some sincere flattery. Can't think of anything? Two good compliments are "Nice gazongas" and "Mind if I walk behind you? I like the view."

SEX. Want to really turn her off? Act like you can't keep it in your pants. Females run from a guy who's intent only on satisfying his carnal desires. You must be clear about your self-control, starting with the very first date. Even before dinner is over, tell her she can be on top.

From left, Jim Carrey, Damon Wayans, and Jeff Goldblum in *Earth Girls Are Easy*, the movie that would lead to Jim's next break.

Out of their alien guises, Jim Carrey, Jeff Goldblum, and Damon Wayans go cruising with Geena Davis and Julie Brown in *Earth Girls Are Easy*.

casting his new comedy show for Fox, *In Living Color*. Wayans suggested his friend Carrey, but Carrey initially wasn't interested.

"I didn't want to do TV," he told *TV Guide*. "I didn't see much there except for *Cheers*."

As he added to *Playboy*, "Most of it is so insulting, so horrifying. I didn't want to be part of anybody's sitcom. They're so terrible. I remember going to auditions and once they asked me what my likes and dislikes were on television. And I said that my dislike *was* television. And that's probably not a good thing to say in a TV audition."

Wayans, however, explained that just by the nature of the show, Carrey wouldn't be stuck playing a single character each week. Still, as the sole white male in the cast, Carrey wanted to avoid what he saw as potential pitfalls for being marginalized as a token character player.

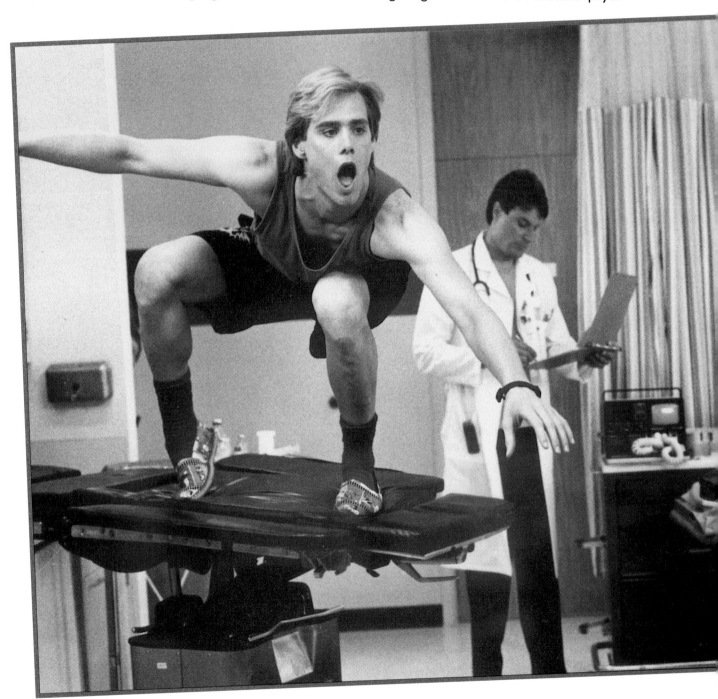

Jim Carrey and Damon Wayans surfed off with most of the laughs in *Earth Girls Are Easy*.

"I went into it sink or swim," he told *Playboy*. "I had never played characters before. I got all kinds of great advice from people, like, 'This is kind of stupid,' and 'Why do you want to be the token white guy?' and all that stuff. It fueled my desire to stand out. Desperation drove me, made all these wild things come out." Or as he told the *Fort Worth Star-Telegram*, "I was hellbent on getting in there and making my own voice heard."

His talent as an impressionist served him well, whether it was a calculat-

ing Vanilla Ice or a juicily lisping Officer Stacey Koon. But there were also his original creations: Vera De Milo, a cross-eyed, whinnying female body-builder who would have to cheat to pass a chromosome test; Grandpa Jack McGee (based on his own alcoholic grandfather), a relative capable of sucking the joy out of any family gathering; and, best known of all, the over-the-top Fire Marshal Bill, a pyromaniac who gave lessons on fire safety while inadvertently setting fires that, in the past, had burned off his hair and lips. The routine drew criticism from various sources for being in poor taste and disrespectful to fire fighters.

"But I had cops come up and thank me," he told *Florida Today*. "They said that ever since *Car 54, Where Are You*, cops have been raked over the coals, and finally the firemen were getting it."

Even as the show pushed an envelope originally pushed by *Saturday Night Live*, Carrey wanted to keep right on pushing, beyond the bounds normally favored by network censors. He continually ran up against stubborn network executives who told him he was going too far. At one point, even Keenen Ivory Wayans agreed with them.

As Carrey told the Portland *Oregonian*, he had come up with a character to mock the strident pro-life forces: a ventriloquist who appears at antiabortion rallies with a puppet that looks like a fetus.

JIM CARREY'S TEN-BEST PICKUP LINES

1. "I can look right up your nose."

2. "I'm wearing dinosaur underwear."

3. "Your hair is the same color as my gerbil."

4. "I can go a whole day without going to the bathroom."

5. "May I buy you a chocolate milk?"

6. "I look familiar. Haven't we met somewhere before?"

7. "I'll lick your hair if you lick mine."

8. "Your eyes are like bowls of Cocoa Puffs."

9. "I have goldfish in my pants."

10. "Mom's place or yours?"

JIM'S ETIQUETTE GUIDE

1. **WHEN YOU FEEL** an explosive fart coming on in public, be considerate enough to light it for the entertainment of all.

2. **THINK OF OTHERS** when belching. Don't leave it at a commonplace "Uurp" when a more creative "Brrrraaaaat" is doable.

3. **A PAPER BAG FILLED WITH DOG SHIT** makes a thoughtful housewarming gift. Simply deposit it on someone's doorstep, light it, ring the doorbell, and run. Capture the moment on videotape as your new friend stamps out the fire.

4. **IF YOU MUST VOMIT** at a dinner party, make sure the white wine comes up with the fish.

5. **COURTESY MEANS** not being afraid to be old-fashioned. Try one of these time-tested party icebreakers:
   * **Tape a Kick Me sign to the fattest guy's butt.**
   * **Lace the punch with LSD.**
   * **Call in a false fire alarm.**
   * **Plant a mike in the bathroom and wire it into your speaker system.**
   * **Announce that the salmon mousse was tainted and drive everybody to the hospital to get their stomachs pumped.**

Here's the crazy crew from *In Living Color*. Top row (left to right), David Alan Grier, Kelly Coffield, Damon Wayans, Keenen Ivory Wayans. Bottom row (left to right), T'Keyah "Crystal" Keymah, Kim Wayans, Tommy Davidson, and Jim Carrey, with one leg out, racing toward his future.

"There's really not that much in this world, except the death of a loved one, that should be taken all that seriously," he told *Saturday Night* magazine. "You can even joke about that if you want to. As far as I'm concerned, if God knows where your heart is, you're all right. I'm not a mean person."

During the hiatus before *In Living Color*'s fourth season, Carrey got the opportunity he'd been waiting for: the chance to star in a movie of his own. Granted, it was an extremely low budget comedy, one that virtually every other comic actor in Hollywood had looked at—and rejected.

But Carrey saw something in *Ace Ventura: Pet Detective*: the chance to exploit his talent for putting an oddball twist on anything he touched, which is exactly how he approached each take of the film. There is not a

As you can see here, Jim's talent for impressions served him well on *In Living Color*.

Finally, Jim broke through. Ace Ventura, you have arrived!

In *Ace Ventura*, Jim gave the "most outrageously mannered comic performance in recent memory." Is that good?

scene, a line reading, even an eyebrow lift that doesn't have some comic backspin on it. It's one of the most outrageously mannered comic performances in recent memory.

"I knew it was either going to be popular or it was going to ruin my career," he says. "Then I wouldn't be able to do another movie for ten years. Every night, the director and I would be writing, looking at each other, saying, 'Where are we, man?' But my stage work is a lot like that. That's where the character comes from: this full-of-shit guy. Every scene that came up, I'd think, What haven't I seen? I wanted to make something different."

As he told the *Fort Worth Star-Telegram*, "Ace is like James Bond meets Jerry Lewis. He's cool, man. He's a hero. He's not a doofus, although he has moments. He's so cool it's ridiculous. I'm a big fan of ridiculousness. I'm not going to be challenging anybody spiritually with this movie, you know?"

At the same time, Carrey was spoofing himself with the part: "It was making fun of my own ego," he told the *Detroit News*. "That's how I wrote the movie. It was, 'If I were getting my way, what would I do?' I'd wanna get the girl and have sex right away. I'd wanna be the guy who has all the smart answers and not think of them on

Jim's face says it all: "I'm a big fan of ridiculousness."

Jim demonstrates his dating tips. Actress Courteney Cox, his costar in *Ace Ventura*, doesn't look too interested. Too bad this shot was taken at the beginning of his demonstration.

It takes courage to be a star; you can't be chicken.

HOW TO TALK WITH YOUR BUTT

Butt talking is an ancient art. Cave paintings discovered in France this year distinctly show early man talking with his butt. Thus, even before the invention of politics, men were talking out of their butts.

It is only in the late twentieth century, our own era, that butts have taken their rightful place in the forefront of modern communications skills. A survey of prominent figures in America today, from Beavis and Butthead to Rush Limbaugh and Jim Carrey, shows that talking butts may well replace talking heads. Now every film student knows that Jim Carrey brought butt talking to the big screen in Ace Ventura: Pet Detective. As with all Jim's humor, he made it look easy. However, aficionados across the country soon found out that talking out of your butt is anything but simple—unless you have a natural flair for it.

With a little practice, this simple guide can have you talking out of your butt with the best of them. And don't let cranky educators or parents deter you. This is an important skill. A career in personnel management or even law could result. So, practice, practice, practice, butt don't forget to have a good time.

1. Face away from the person you are addressing. This is important. For those of you who didn't flunk geometry—and you know who you are—face 180 degrees from your interlocutor, if you didn't flunk English, you know who that is.

2. Bend over. Note: Do not accept this advice in any other context. Also, do not practice when guys who like Liza Minnelli records are in the room.

3. Reach around and grab your cheeks. Not those cheeks. The other cheeks. Riiiiight. This should be easy unless you are very fat or flunked gym.

4. Use the sort of voice you think your butt would use if it could talk for itself. This is the really hard part. If you didn't flunk literature, use your imagination and think of the literary character your butt would probably be. Do you have a lisping, French, Madame Bovary butt? Is it a nervous, elderly, Miss Havisham butt? Could a tough-talking, cool, Sam Spade butt be right up your alley? You decide. When in doubt, start with a slightly high pitched version of your speaking voice and let your butt find its own voice.

5. While moving your cheeks back and forth to simulate mouth movements, let your butt do the talking. Begin with the traditional "Let me ass you something" and then improvise. You will no doubt be pleasantly surprised to find that most butts have something to say, given the opportunity. Unless you totally flunked vocabulary, you can pepper your talk with phrases like "If I don't get what I want, I'll set off a big stink around here" or "I've got something to say, and it's a real gas."

6. Butt do's and don'ts. Observe butt etiquette. You wouldn't belch in someone's face, would you? Don't worry if your butt is more outspoken than you are. Many butts are downright insulting. Maybe they just weren't reared right. Have fun and don't worry about making an ass of yourself.

the bus going home. And that's Ace."

Nor was he putting pressure on himself. As he and director Tom Shadyac rewrote the script even as they were filming it, Carrey purposely chose not to relate the fun he was having to expectations about the movie and his career. He had played that game before and paid the emotional toll when things didn't pan out.

"If I went into *Ace Ventura* thinking, 'This is my shot,' I'd be dead," he told the *Fort Worth Star-Telegram*. "There's no way. You'd put too much pressure on it. It wouldn't be fun anymore. You just get in there and play."

He kept things light on the set, particularly when working with costar Sean Young, who was still notorious for her high profile tabloid battle with actor James Woods.

"As soon as she showed up on the set," he told Knight-Ridder newspapers, "in front of everybody, I said, 'We're not gonna put up with any of your shit, Sean.' She laughed, and it let the pressure off, because everybody was waiting for this witch to show up."

After *Ace Ventura* earned $12 million in its opening weekend, Jim Carrey could stand on any desk he wanted to.

Jim Carrey's main squeeze, Lauren Holly.

He also brought along a trademark gag: "Until *Ace Ventura*" he told *Playboy*, "no actor had considered talking through his ass."

The cheeky technique emerged a couple of years earlier, during his stint on *In Living Color*. One day on the set, Carrey disagreed with writer-producer Keenen Ivory Wayans over the quality of the script. Wayans maintained that the script was funny and commanded Carrey to read it. So Carrey turned around, bent over, put his hands on his butt, and used it to read the disputed sketch.

Ace Ventura was released in February 1994 and grossed a startling $12 million in its first weekend, topping the box-office charts for several weeks, to the

befuddlement of critics and studio executives alike, all of whom dismissed the film.

There is the story, for instance, of a studio boss who, after the highly unexpected success of *Ace Ventura*, ordered all of his executives to go see the movie in a theater with an audience, then come back to explain to him why they hadn't made the picture themselves. Of course, the studio boss missed the point entirely. It wasn't the movie that was such a hit; it was Jim Carrey! As he told Canada's *Saturday Night* magazine, his appeal was that "I have the face of John-boy Walton and the brain of Salvador Dali."

On opening weekend, Carrey was in Atlanta. He summoned stand-up friend Wayne Flemming, and the

Jim was paid bird seed for *Ace Ventura* and *The Mask*, but that would soon change.

Lauren Holly turned down the romantic lead in *Ace Ventura*, which Courteney Cox happily took in her stead.

Jim and Lauren Holly at the premiere for *The Mask*.

Here are Jim and Lauren at the premiere for *Dumb and Dumber.*

Jim and Lauren are looking spiffy at the American Film Institute dinner honoring Steven Spielberg.

Who's that blonde Jim Carrey's with? It's Lauren Holly again. Can't fool you.

FAME HAS ITS REWARDS

Most celebrities haul in the big bucks by making product endorsements. Jim Carrey is no exception. Of course, there are levels of celebrity and, therefore, levels of product endorsement.

Before Ace Ventura, Jim Carrey couldn't pay for a dozen clown noses with the money he made on endorsements. The following is a list of his top endorsements before Ace and the money he earned plugging those products:

> Adam Ant Makeup—$39
>
> Bulgarian Fat-Free Chewing Gum—$42
>
> Barry Manilow Air Fresheners—$128

After becoming the highest-paid film comedy star in the world, Jim could write his own ticket with advertisers. Look for Jim endorsing these products on your home tube soon:

> Cyanide-Free Nuclear-Strength Tylenol— $250,000
>
> Mouse X Tablets: for up to eight hours of non-mouse-like speech—$75,000
>
> Swanson's Rhino Pot Pie/Endangered Gourmet Delicacy—$150,000
>
> Barry Manilow Air Fresheners—$128 (still under contract)

pair began touring Atlanta, scoping out movie theaters to see his name on the marquees. To their surprise, they also saw lengthy lines of people waiting to get in to the theaters beneath those marquees. When he heard the grosses the following Monday, Flemming told Knight-Ridder newspapers, he turned to Carrey and said, "That's it—you're a big star now."

"I don't believe it," Carrey said, dazed.

But *Ace Ventura* was made at a personal cost. His marriage to Melissa was shattered. He blames himself. At night, he says, he simply wants to be left alone to stalk the living room and wrestle with new ideas. He has no choice.

"I'm a hard guy to live with," he told the *New York Times*. "I'm like a caged animal. It's hard for me to come down from what I do. It's like being an astronaut." Melissa wanted him to land his mental spacecraft every night, but he couldn't always bring it down. She would tell him, "You must come home and put your feet back on the ground and take your garbage out like everyone else, or I can't be married to you."

She laments, "Basically, he called my bluff."

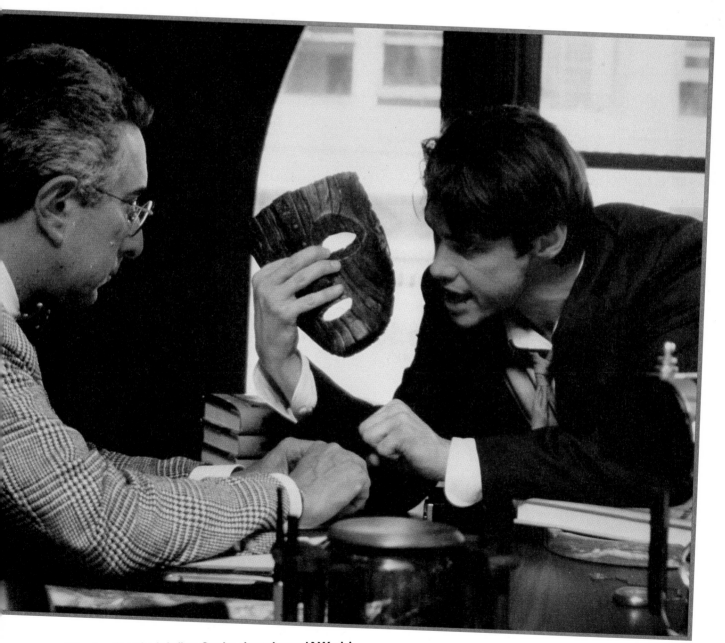

Why doesn't anybody believe Stanley about the mask? We do!

JIM CARREY'S
HEALTH AND BEAUTY SECRETS

CONTRACEPTION AND SAFE SEX

Jim's foolproof recipe! Orange juice. Not before sex. Not after sex. Instead of sex.

PLAGUE

Avoid it—like the plague.

ULCERS

Don't get them. Be a carrier.

BOTTOM BURPING

Don't fight them. Light them.

ORAL HYGIENE

Brush teeth thoroughly as follows: Brush up, brush down, then shake your toothbrush out. Then you do the hokeypokey and you turn yourself around. That's what it's all about.

TONGUE DEPRESSORS

When your tongue is a little manic and you feel the need for a downer, frost seems to work well.

EYE IRRITANTS

Jim likes breath spray.

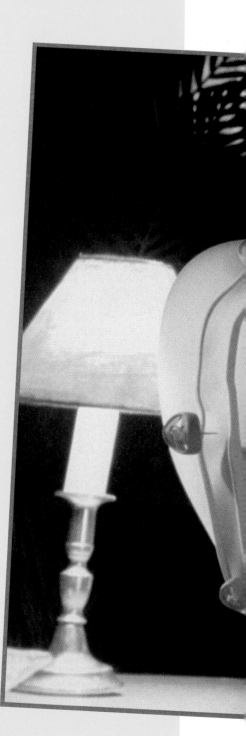

Jim *exploding* **with special effects.**

"It was really tough being married," Carrey told *Parade* magazine, "because I'm in love with my work and it's hard not to be jealous of that. It's hard for anybody who's with me not to feel starved for affection when I'm making love to my ideas. I can see a real challenge in my life will be to settle myself down enough to be with someone. Maybe it's not meant to be for me."

He claims that he doesn't have time for anything else in his life right now except his daughter (eight-year-old Jane) and his work. Unless he's filming, he spends two or three days a week with Jane, making her his top priority.

Nevertheless, he has made time for one woman in his life: *Dumb and Dumber* costar Lauren Holly, who, incidentally, had nothing whatsoever to do with the breakup of Carrey's marriage. They did meet before the breakup; she was up for the part eventually played by Courteney Cox in *Ace Ventura: Pet Detective*, but she

When *Mask* director Chuck Russell told Jim that he would explode with special effects, he wasn't kidding.

turned it down! They didn't begin dating for almost a year after Carrey left Melissa.

Not that Carrey was celibate once he split with his wife. "I had suddenly become a big star," he told *Rolling Stone*, "and I realized—not trying to be egotistical—I could get laid every hour on the hour. I quickly found out that I'm not the dog that I thought it was maybe possible for me to be. The bottom line is, I really want to love somebody. I do. I just don't know if it's possible forever and ever."

Except for one heralded breakup—and patch-up—he and Lauren Holly have been together now for more than a year, with no end in sight. And they seem to be everywhere together. And lookin' mighty good, too. Or at least dressed real well.

He had his "dog" days during the making of *The Mask*, the movie he jumped into right after *Ace Ventura*. It was an adaptation of a cult comic book written expressly with Carrey's elastic face and frame in mind.

Poor Stanley Ipkiss, if he only knew what was waiting for him in the next picture.

At this moment, Stanley's doing fine without his mask. That's Cameron Diaz with him; we knew you wanted to know.

And here she is again. And what's he lookin' at?

Nobody can tango like _The Mask_.

"I never had a stronger instinct about a guy than I did about Jim," director Chuck Russell told the *Detroit News.* "I went to him with six panels from the comic and said, 'This is an archetype. Then we'll explode it with special effects and you'll be hysterical.'"

The film blended a pair of Carrey performances: as the nebbishy bank clerk Stanley Ipkiss and as the Mask, the incredibly hyperactive superhero he became whenever he donned a mysterious wooden mask.

"There's a lot of my father in Stanley," he told the *Detroit News.* "For me it's an opportunity to do, hopefully, a three-dimensional character that doesn't rely on tricks. The most important part of this film for me was to create a character in Stanley Ipkiss who is entertain-

Ah, come on! Put it on!

Here's Jim with Cameron Diaz offscreen during the premiere party for *The Mask.*

Here Jim wishes he was with Cameron Diaz. Or any sane person.

ing on his own: 'Hey, I could go a whole movie with this character.' I love Stanley Ipkiss because he's a good guy who doesn't let life warp him. He really is the hero of the film. He has the Mask inside him before he even finds it."

Besides the computer-generated special-effects imagery, the film featured Carrey made up as a bald-domed, earless skull with mammoth choppers and skin that ran to a brilliant avocado green.

"That makeup really brings the character to life," he said. "It's such an amazing design. You get those big teeth in and it's like you're a cartoon. As soon as I was made up, I became 'The Mask.' I could feel the character just burst through me. Basically, it was a joygasm, and that's what 'The Mask' is; he's just pure adrenaline. It felt schizophrenic because, on one level, I'm this sweet inno-cent guy, and on another level, I'm this wound-up ball of spontaneous combustion."

Creating the look of The Mask required a four-hour makeup time each day: "You just go insane," he says. "Basically I would black out. I'd close my eyes and wander off in my imagination—with occasional cigarette breaks."

As *The Mask* was being released and Carrey made the rounds to talk to the press to promote the film, he was amused at the press attention being paid to the news that he would receive $7 million for his next film.

"Well, they're going to talk about that, but hey—there are people making more money than me. They're carbon-based life-forms. I'm a carbon-based life-form. Why not? A couple of movies in, they'll forget about me. But it's happened to me in such an outrageous manner and has accelerated at such an incredible rate—it's like Cinderella. Except it's never going to be mid-night."

"Isn't it incredible?" he said to Knight-Ridder newspa-pers. "There are times when you say, 'What the hell is going on?' "

As he told the *Detroit News*, "It's great, it really is. I can't downplay it. It's like we won the election."

It was a good thing, he told *Newsweek*, that success didn't come until he was ready to handle it: "I'm just really glad it happened the way it did, because if it had happened when I was twenty-one, I probably would have blown my brains out. Unless I had gone through all

Jim Carrey is seen here with his manager, Buddy Morra. With the kind of money his management team is bringing him now, Carrey apparently feels he needs to do more than kiss his manager's feet; he needs to eat them!

Yes, indeedy, he sure wears better duds now, and that's no bull.

SISBERT AND EKEL

An Interview With Jim Carrey

SISBERT: Jim.

CARREY: Please call me Bob.

SISBERT: Okay, Bob, I understand that you turned down the Schwarzenegger role in *Last Action Hero*.

CARREY: Yes. Red Buttons and Dom DeLuise advised me to wait for a role with more meat . . . and possibly some potatoes.

EKEL: Yes. Well, Bob, Steven Spielberg——

CARREY: Hold it right there! No questions about Steven Spielberg. I had E.T. down cold, and he chose a puppet! Let him live with the consequences.

SISBERT: But, Mr. Carrey, *E.T.* made millions of dollars.

CARREY: The guy in the rubber suit cleared that kind of dough?

EKEL: No. Not the puppet! The movie!

CARREY: Oh, I never saw it.

EKEL: Earlier in your career, you turned down the Jennifer Beals role in *Flashdance*.

CARREY: Yes, my personal trainer advised me that the dance numbers might hurt my hair.

EKEL: Do you regret that decision?

CARREY: Yes, I do. As you know, I have been a disco cage dancer for many years, and I take it quite seriously. I also dance at bar mitzvahs and small private parties. But I find that I have little time for that now.

SISBERT: What was that noise?

CARREY: I have a duck in my pants. Little Duckie, Little Duckie . . .

SISBERT: Mr. Carrey. Jim——er, Bob——

CARREY: Yes, Gene.

SISBERT: Is it true that a squabble over money kept you from starring in the latest James Bond movie?

CARREY: No, Pierce Brosnan threatened to rearrange my face. Which is strange, since I can do that without Pierce.

EKEL: Isn't Michael Keaton also mad at you for landing the role of the Riddler in *Batman Forever*?

CARREY: Roger, everyone in Los Angeles is mad at me. But I'm able to use their anger. To turn it around and become a love boy.

SISBERT: You've been interested in getting involved in another animation project since *Mask*. Is there anything on the horizon?

CARREY: Absolutely, and I don't think the studio will mind if I tell you. I will be the voice of the Kevin Costner character in Oliver Stone's animated version of *JFK*.

SISBERT: No kidding. Is animation your first love?

CARREY: No. Twizzlers would be my first love . . . No. Actually strawberry milk shakes would be first, and Twizzlers would be my second or maybe my fourth love. I guess animation would be my third love.

SISBERT: Do you do any special facial exercises?

CARREY: Yes. I have a face trainer. But you're getting into a personal area here.

SISBERT: Are you part of the Hollywood party scene?

CARREY: Yes, Mike Ovitz and I regularly play miniature golf. Tonight I'm skeet shooting with Bette Midler.

EKEL: Who would you say your biggest influences are?

CARREY: Definitely Pete Best . . . Oh, let's see. Martha Raye, Yosemite Sam, and of course, Larry Storch.

that disappointment, I don't think I would feel like I deserve it. As it is, I still every once in a while think, 'Ooh, what if they take it away?' "

Nor, he continued, would he let it change him: "I have a bigger house now and I wear OK duds, but I always cringe when I get invitations to things. I don't want to be seen going to Planet Hollywood and that kind of stuff. Someone who works for me just told me to have my colors done, and it's nice they were thinking of me but I don't see that happening. I've seen guys I've worked with get a show and the next thing you know they're pulling up to the Comedy Store in a big car. I'd rather keep my cards in a little bit and see how things turn out. Ultimately what you're being paid for is that spark, that kind of believing in magic. People want to see somebody who still believes in magic."

But in Hollywood, there is black magic, too. Around the time of *The Mask's* release, an opportunistic video company resurrected *High Strung*, in which Carrey had appeared in a couple of brief scenes in 1989 as a favor for a friend, Steve Oedekerk, with the promise that his name or likeness wouldn't be mentioned in the advertising. But when Carrey zoomed in popularity, the pro-ducer pulled the movie off the shelf and released it on video with a garish ad campaign prominently featuring Carrey.

"I did one day of shooting and specifically asked them not to use my name or likeness in the products," he told *USA Today.* "It's a lesson learned. You can't do favors for friends with your talent, with your career. Some people just can't help themselves."

The Mask proved to be an even bigger hit—and turned Carrey into an even bigger star. "If New Line Cinema's *The Mask* doesn't turn out to be one of the summer's smash movies, it won't be because all the necessary calculations haven't been made," wrote Roger Fristoe in the *Louisville Courier-Journal.*

Even as *The Mask* was climbing the box-office charts, Carrey was trying to cling to a self-image as a normal guy.

"It is weird," he told *Playboy,* "very, very weird. My life is still a

Here's a shot from the movie *High Strung*, made in 1989, but only released on video when Jim hit it big. Jim has a cameo.

La "Kook"aracha.

string of embarrassments. I go to premieres and try to make a cool exit and the limo driver locks his keys in the car and it's running and he's trying to pick the lock while I'm standing there and the theater is emptying out. Real cool."

Carrey was still working out on a regular basis in comedy clubs, testing himself, honing his abilities.

"It's a chance for me to kind of keep connected to what's real," he told Knight-Ridder newspapers, "because if you get stuck behind movie cameras all the time, after a while, the reaction isn't the same, it's not real. The stage is where you create. Standing up in front of 3,000 people, you're forced to come up with something. You force yourself out on a limb that way. It's like getting started over in show business every night, getting cursed out by the audience and all that. I had some wild nights."

He was offered *Dumb and Dumber* shortly after *Ace Ventura* opened, with its impressive box-office display. Carrey was able to command $7 million from New Line Cinema, which had paid him $450,000 for *The Mask*.

"I was first attracted to this film because of its title," he told *Parade*. "I read the script and liked the idea of working with someone and not carrying the whole film by myself. Jeff [Daniels] is a quality actor, and at this

No wonder Jim is singing—and here are some of his greatest hits: "Ace Ventura Highway"; "It Isn't Easy Being Green" (with special guest artist, Kermit the Frog); "Dumb Dee Dumb Dumb. . . . Dumb Dee Dumb Dumb DAAAAAAAH!" (the theme from Dragnet), the original soundtrack of *Dumb and Dumber* includes Jeff Daniels's performance of "Classical Gas." (This album is available exclusively on vinyl.)

Jim said he wanted to work with Jeff Daniels in *Dumb and Dumber*. Or maybe he just wanted a ride in the "Mutt-Cutts" truck.

Not only is Jim's goofball hairdo on display in *Dumb and Dumber;* so is his famous chipped tooth.

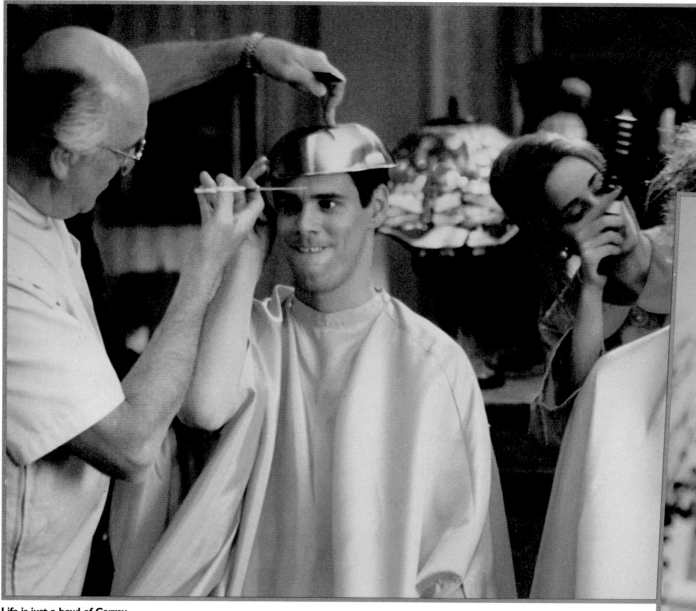

Life is just a bowl of Carrey.

Befuddlement becomes them. Jim and *Dumb and Dumber* costar Jeff Daniels each have his own way of expressing total confusion.

Not only did we have a good time in *Dumb and Dumber*; so did Jim and Jeff.

point I want to work with people who can challenge me to be better."

On *Dumb and Dumber*, he uncovered the chipped tooth he'd had since second grade. As he told *Nickelodeon* magazine, he was laying his head on his desk in detention one day when a friend "decided to do a running cannonball on my head."

Besides the tooth, Carrey went to goofy lengths with his hair for *Dumb and Dumber*: "My hair is basically a bowl cut. It's got a little Spock going on, and a little ancient-monk thing. I was trying to figure out what would make me look dumbest. The short bangs seem to do it nicely."

The story is about two intensely dim friends who travel from the East Coast to Aspen to return a lost suitcase, unaware that it contains a fortune in ransom money.

"It's 'Of Mice and Men', basically, " Carrey told the *Detroit News*.

As he told *Playboy*, "The picture is about two stupid guys who become friends. I met Jeff Daniels and we had immediate rapport. I had casting approval, so I fought for him. But it wasn't what the marketing geniuses had in mind. They wanted someone with an MTV profile, whatever that means. Jeff is a wonderful actor and my favorite from the start. The idea that I could play this wild character and work with an actor that I could learn something from was great. It's really fun to watch someone like Jeff totally let go. We had a great time."

Carrey worked with the film's director and writers to sharpen the script and add to the laughs: "We just kept pecking away, making it funnier and funnier and funnier. Even though the characters have screwed-up morals, we wanted to help bring out their innocence, since there is a wholesome purity about them."

How to play dumb? "When the cameras roll," Carrey says, "we just get the glassy 'I just ate lead paint for breakfast' look. We don't gear up for it. We gear down."

The film also brought to light his romantic involvement with actress Lauren Holly, his costar and love interest in the film. "It sounds clichéd," he told *USA Today*. "Everybody goes 'Oh gosh, the leading lady and the leading man,' but the fact is that if you're making movies back-to-back, that's where you meet people."

To Carrey, the $7 million payday for *Dumb and Dumber* was startling, considering that he wasn't complaining about what he had made on *Ace Ventura* or *The Mask*: respectively, $350,000 and $450,000.

"That was a healthy sum of money," Carrey told *Parade* of the *Ace* and *Mask* paydays. "When I started out, I'd drive 100 miles to do my act for free.

But the times were definitely changing. Soon Carrey was so sought after that when a spate of agency talent raids made news in early 1995, it was rumored (falsely,

Jim Carrey has been called many names.
WE HID TWENTY OF THEM IN THIS PUZZLE. SEE IF YOU CAN FIND THEM.

N	I	T	W	I	T	D	D	U	D
I	O	D	I	D	I	O	T	D	U
N	B	O	Z	O	B	R	A	I	N
C	M	P	D	I	P	K	B	M	D
O	U	E	N	L	Z	E	X	W	E
M	D	T	U	N	E	R	D	I	R
P	T	W	T	W	Q	H	V	T	H
O	W	E	D	U	N	C	E	Z	E
O	I	R	N	I	N	N	Y	A	A
P	T	P	A	I	R	H	E	A	D

Here's another look at Jim's hearthrob, Lauren, along with comedienne **Teri Garr** in a scene from *Dumb and Dumber.*

In this shot, that "wholesome purity" they were after sure came through, especially on Jeff Daniels's face.

Val Kilmer plays Batman, and Chris O'Donnell plays Robin, but who cares? Everybody went to *Batman Forever* to see Jim Carrey play the Riddler.

as it turned out) that his agency, United Talent Agency, had assigned someone to watch him twenty-four hours a day, to fend off unwanted advances by poachers from other agencies.

No wonder the rumor had flashed. In early 1995, Carrey was making headlines for the startling videocassette sales of *The Mask*, which were reaching 10 million units. At that same time, *Ace Ventura: Pet Detective* had hit the hot rotation on HBO. Soon after, he was a Golden Globe and People's Choice Award nominee.

Even as the publicity storm was flying around Carrey, the long-rumored third *Batman* film was in the works. For years it had been assumed that Robin Williams would play the Riddler if *Batman 3* ever got off the ground. But once a script was developed and reworked, and a director (Joel Schumacher) signed, Williams balked, demanding more script work before he would commit.

Instead, the filmmakers turned to the comedy supernova of the year. It seemed the perfect blend: Carrey gave the new *Batman* some much-needed marquee power, while the *Batman* role offered Carrey credibility in a major franchise film.

It also gave him the chance to act opposite serious performers: classically trained Val Kilmer and Oscar-winner Tommy Lee Jones.

The villain roles in the *Batman* movies have proved to be the series' most galvanizing. And as most any actor who has worked with Tommy Lee Jones can attest, there is hardly a better scene-stealer in the business. Who would come out on top between Jones as Harvey "Two Face" Dent and Carrey as the Riddler? Even before the movie opened, the film's director, Joel Schumacher, told *Rolling Stone*, "Tommy is used to stealing the show. He definitely met his match here and many times was surprised by it."

There's really no question about it. For all the attention Val Kilmer got as the new replacement Batman (for Michael Keaton), for all the ink generated by the addition of Robin (Chris O'Donnell) to the cast, and for all the thespian reputation brought to bear by Tommy Lee Jones, it was Jim Carrey everyone was talking about.

Jim Carrey's Foul Play— A Mix 'N' Match Game

Match the disgusting trait with your favorite character from Jim's movies or with revolting morons you actually know.

There are no wrong answers, so take your finger out of your nose, grab a pencil, and go!

A.	Frozen snot on face	1.	Jim in *DUMB AND DUMBER*
B.	Hidden wienie	2.	Jim in *ACE VENTURA*
C.	Profound diarrhea	3.	Sean Young in *ACE VENTURA*
D.	Massive teeth	4.	Jim in *THE MASK*
E.	Lush nostril hair	5.	Your father after a six-pack
F.	Green skin	6.	You at eighteen
G.	Binaca-blinded eyes	7.	Jeff Daniels in *DUMB AND DUMBER*
H.	Noxious-gas emissions	8.	The terrier in *THE MASK*
I.	Scary, gaunt face	9.	Strom Thurmond
J.	Projectile vomiting	10.	Fire Marshal Bill
		11.	Your mother after happy hour

ANSWERS: A-1; B-3; C-7; D-8; E-1; F-6; G-1; H-5; I-9; J-11

The real matchup was between Oscar-winner Tommy Lee Jones as Harvey "Two Face" Dent and Jim Carrey's Riddler.

The Batman Villain Hall of Fame and I.Q. Test

Match the correct description in the column on the left with the appropriate pictures on the following pages. You get one point for each right answer and no points, dummy, for wrong answers. The answers can be found in the tiny print on page 106.

Sexiest

Most elegantly dressed

Biggest mouth

Most schizophrenic

Best leer

Nicholson as the Joker

Carrey as the Riddler

Tommy Lee Jones as Two Face

Michelle Pfeiffer as Catwoman

[Answer: If you matched Jim Carrey to all the descriptions on page 102, you win; this is his scrapbook. Whaddya expect?]

Danny DeVito as the Penguin

An impossibly skinny Jim painted himself into that Riddler costume and made everyone forget about Frank Gorshin—or Robin Williams, for that matter. Slithering, skittering, giggling, cackling, and snickering, he was the wild card in the big comic-book extravaganza, with a copper-colored crew cut and sly mask highlighting the madness in his eyes.

His role, like all of the characters in *Batman Forever*, was underwritten. It required him to create something from inside, something insanely entertaining. It helped that he is completely at ease when performing. He once told the *New York Times*, "I've never had any trouble being in front of a camera. I used to get into arguments with my acting coach. He told me if I can't do something in front of my family, in front of people I love, then I'll never be able to pull it off in front of the camera. And I told him he was absolutely wrong. There are many things I could do before a camera that I can't do before my family. When the camera goes on, hey, desperation steps in. You better do something interesting."

"I like the idea of working with people who scare me," he says, "who scare me creatively and make me stay on my game."

It's part of his plan to move into serious roles, such as the one he played as an alcoholic son in the television movie *Doing Time on Maple Drive* for director Ken Olin of *thirtysomething* fame. Olin, in fact, auditioned Carrey, not knowing he was a comedian: "I'd never have imagined he was a comedic actor," Olin told *TV Guide*. "He gave a very honest reading. It was so sad. I think he understands the part personally."

"Comics are really good at drama if they can drop the façade long enough," Carrey says. "The audience cares more about a guy who makes them laugh. They like a good man who feels down rather than a down

The Jim Carrey IQ Test

INSTRUCTIONS: Sharpen a number 2 pencil.
Take two aspirin.
Answer the following two questions.
Go make number two.

(Actually, there are five questions. Do your best.)

VOCABULARY

Choose the pair of words that best completes the following sentences:

1. I _____ therefore I _____.
   A. think, am
   B. think, suck
   C. think, dunno?
2. All _____ _____.
   A. for one
   B. About Eve
   C. righty then
3. In _____ _____.
   A. like Flynn
   B. dagada bagivita
   C. Living Color

MULTIPLE CHOICE

Choose the best answer:

4. You finally get a date with someone you have been strongly attracted to. You insist on seeing *The Mask* with them, even though you have seen it forty-nine times. Your new friend doesn't get it. You_____.
   A. gently deconstruct the back story while explicating the sight gags and many references to classic films.
   B. kill them.
   C. play it over and over until they scream.

MATH

Solve the following problems:

5. If there were two stars in *Dumb and Dumber* and three major bathroom scenes, how many girls on the Swedish bikini team needed oiling?_____

man who feels downer. There's more value in a character who has pain and tries to get around it rather than wallow in it."

As he told *USA Today*, "If I do a serious movie, I wanna bring some humor to it. It always bothers me when I see a movie where actors are, like, just down to begin with. The James Dean type of thing, which everybody seems to want to be, I don't think works for me."

"*Batman Forever*," he told *Premiere* magazine, is "a little more colorful, a little more fun" than its predecessors. "I don't think it takes itself as seriously, but it's still got an edge to it. And it has me in it. That's the difference."

In his one serious role to date, the television movie *Doing Time on Maple Drive*, Jim Carrey acquitted himself well.

Jim Carrey is dogging it in a publicity shot from *The Mask* with **Milo**, his hilarious costar.

How goofy would TV be if Jim Carrey ran his own network? Well, it's time to tune in, because . . .

JCTV Is Now on the Air!

6 AM **FUTURE FARMER—Instructional**
The effect of white noise herbicides on hog clones.

6:30 **THE SUBLIMINAL SHOW—Content unknown**

7 AM **FUN WITH JELL-O—Instructional** *1:00*
Host chef: Snoop Doggy Dogg.

8 AM **CULTURE HOUR** *1:00*
The Richard Nixon Mime Troupe at the Kennedy Center.
Host: Don Rickles.

9 AM **THE GRAVITY-FREE GAME SHOW—Game** *1:00*
Floating contestants dressing each other, making malted milks, and attempting other
simple tasks for worthless prizes.
Hosts: Regis and Kathie Lee.

10 AM **NINJA KNOWS BEST—Comedy**
David Carradine as a retired ninja in suburban Milwaukee.

10:30 AM **NUN BUT THE BEST—Comedy** *1:00*
A delightful show that's fun for the whole family. It's the story of a nun who ends up
coaching the Dallas Cowboys. Ellen Degeneres, Chris Farley, and Andy Rooney.

11:30 AM **MOZART IN NASHVILLE—Comedy**
Wolfgang Mozart is suddenly transported to Nashville when he accidentally plays a
country-and-western tune on his piano. Mozart: Jerry Seinfeld, backed up by the
"Wolf Gang" of Pamela Sue Anderson, Fran Drescher, and Connie Chung.

Noon **AUSTRALIAN MEAT HOCKEY—Sports Special** *4:00*
Canberra vs. Perth.

4 PM **BOWLING FOR FOOD—Game** *1:00*
Families strike out for three squares and spares on this Spam-sponsored show.

5 PM **THE MESSIAH COLONY—Movie (1995)** *2:30*
Two thousand years in the present, Jesus Christ squares off against Nazi Ants in the
ultimate conflict of good and evil. Jesus: Luke Perry. Nazi Ants: themselves.

7:30   **HELEN KELLER IN OUTER SPACE—Drama** *1:00*

A sci-fi thriller about Helen Keller's adventurous attempt at groping her way to the Andromeda galaxy. Helen: Heather Locklear. Captain Jack: Jerry Van Dyke.

8:30   **GLEN CAMPBELL IN ISRAEL—Special** *1:00*

Together with Charo and Drew Barrymore, the "Wichita Lineman" explores Israel in song and dance. Songs include: "Rhinestone Rabbi," "By the Time I Get to Jaffa," and "Hava Nagela," sung with the Children of the Tel Aviv School of the Tiny Torah.

9:30   **BOB HOPE AND HIS GALAXY OF STARS—Variety** *1:30*

America's favorite comedian entertains the astronauts and scientists aboard the space shuttle. Loni Anderson, Buddy Hackett, M. C. Hammer, and Judge Ito.

11 PM   **DEADLINE NEWS—News and information**

The award-winning computer-generated anchor team of "Chip" Holliday and Joy Stick with Native American weatherman Black Cloud and sports mime Biff Peters.

11:30   **JIM NABORS SINGS THE BLUES—Special** *1:00*

Jim "Gomer Pyle" Nabors gets down and belts the blues as only he can. Lee Majors, Garrett Morris, and Courtney Love. Songs include: "I Seem To Have Lost My Job."

12:30   **DICK CLARK'S ROCKIN' TUESDAY EVE—Music** *1:50*

The Sewer Babies farewell concert. The group that put Jefferson City, Missouri, on the map rocks out. Songs include: "Puke Machine," "Heavy Metal Pants," from their rock opera *School Sucks*.

2:20   **MEATLINE—Educational** *1:00*

Ted Koppel hosts a tour of the Barbeque Hall of Fame in Pug, Ohio.

3:20   **ACE VENTURA VII: THE JOURNEY HOME—Movie rerun** *2:40*

Ace helps Lassie retrieve stick. Ace: Jim Carrey. Lassie: Milo.

Of his character, the Riddler, he told *Premiere*, "I think the Riddler would probably take mass transit just to fuck with people, you know what I mean? Just to be the loud one or the one with the music. The one with the bad breath."

Batman Forever had the biggest opening weekend in Hollywood history, taking in an incredible $53.3 million, topping the previous record of $50.2 million set by *Jurassic Park*. How much of that was due to the casting of Jim Carrey as the Riddler will never be known, but it certainly didn't hurt having someone in the cast who had already racked up $550 million in worldwide box-office receipts for three films in 1994.

Miami Dolphins quarterback Dan Marino is smirking. At the time they made *Ace Ventura* together, Marino had a bigger career than Jim. But Jim's smiling back; he knows.

The fact is, reputations aside, Jim Carrey was the only proven box-office draw among all of the leads.

With that thought in mind and expecting *Batman Forever* to open strongly, Columbia/TriStar chairman Mark Canton moved boldly and decisively to snare Jim Carrey for a comedy titled *Cable Guy*, offering him $20 million and fifteen percent of the gross. The guaranteed nature of the deal commits Carrey to begin filming in December 1995, with a release date of summer 1996. Carrey had already turned down $18 million to star in a movie called *The Thief of Santa Monica*. Soon after the *Cable Guy* deal was signed, Carrey picked up another $20 million for a film called *Liar, Liar*.

With this kind of money, Carrey is setting the new gold standard among actors' salaries in Hollywood. By the time *The Mask II* comes out, Jim Carrey will probably be running Hollywood. Perhaps he'll be running his own television network: all Jim Carrey, all the time!

But even as *Batman Forever* was arriving in theaters, Carrey was still in front of cameras shooting *Ace Ventura: When Nature Calls*. When he signed for it, he told the *Detroit News*, "I'm looking forward to getting back to the character. I have such fun doing it: 'Okay, guys—Ace can catch bullets in his teeth.' And we'd make him do it."

The production, however, had well-publicized problems. Carrey suffered major disagreements with director Tom DeCerchio. As tensions flared, Elite model Georgianna Robertson, who had been cast in a prominent role, fell victim to the problems and quit after one day. Then, while on location in San Antonio, Texas, Carrey's problems with DeCerchio became so acute that Carrey refused to leave his trailer. Eventually, DeCerchio was fired and Steve Oedekerk, an old friend of Carrey's and a writer from *In Living Color*, was brought in to direct.

That hunger to perform, to wring the maximum laughter from an audience, hasn't abated: "I think to be a great comic you have to want to express something," Carrey told *Parade*. "And you have to be a serious person to want that. When people meet me for the first time, they usually say, 'Oh, you're so different from what I expected.' I tell them, 'I'm not out of my mind today.' I have a side that I can turn on in a second and have a blast but that comes from my need to escape my seriousness."

He needs that outlet, that chance to burn off excess energy. As he told *TV Guide*, "Even if something should happen to me, and—heaven forbid—all I could move was my baby finger, a few months later people would be saying, 'Hey, you gotta go down to the club to see what Carrey is doing with his finger, man. It's weird!'"

No doubt Carrey was thrilled at becoming the highest-paid comedian in Hollywood history with his $20 million paydays for *Cable Guy* and *Liar, Liar*, but the money he received for agreeing to do *The Mask II* surely meant the most to him. He signed a contract to make the movie in late 1994 for what seemed at the time to be the astronomical figure of $10 million.

JIM CARREY'S LAST WILL AND TESTAMENT

I, Jim Carrey, being of some mind and warped body, do hereby certify that what follows constitutes my Last Will and Testament. In the event that any of my heirs wish to contest this document, I authorize my attorney, Alan Dershowitz, to appear with them in public, which should put a quick halt to the proceedings.

ITEM 1: I leave my Riddler outfit; my skintight Riddler outfit; my shockingly revealing, modesty exploding skintight Riddler outfit with detachable appendages and butt enhancements, to Alex Trebek of *Jeopardy*, in the hope that just once he'll appear before an audience looking like a doofus. While he may make a living from knowing all the answers, it's the Riddler who asks the questions.

ITEM 2: I leave my Fireman Bob flame-retardant fireman's uniform to Mr. Wizard with the desire that it will offer him the same quality protection that it afforded me when he mixes toxic chemicals and nuclear wastes on *Nickelodeon*.

ITEM 3: My dog, Milo, from *The Mask*, I bequeath to serve as the talent agent for the winner of a "pee-down" tournament between Murray (*Mad About You*), Eddie (*Frasier*), Mort (*Bud Lite*), Dogbert (*Dilbert*), and Shithead (*The Jerk*). To be held at the New Orleans Superdome, this "Battle of the Bladder in Loo'siana" will be a WWF-style steel hydrant match, with the first mutt to wet all the others being declared the champion canine sidekick.

ITEM 4: I leave my facial contortions to Hollywood's George Hamilton, who, through decades of exposure on film, has developed a range of expressions that runs from A to B.

ITEM 5: From *Dumb and Dumber*, I leave my short, straight bangs, buck teeth, and innate ability to carry on ordinary social discourse to Kato Kaelin. To make it on the silver screen it is not enough to be a run-of-the-mill ignoramus; a successful moron must truly work at his trade and not rely solely on his God-given talent as a mental defective.

ITEM 6: I leave my slickly coiffed, pompadour-style hairdo from *Ace Ventura* in equal parts to boxing promoter Don King, who has never fully recovered from his childhood reenactment of Benjamin Franklin's kite-flying discovery of electricity, and to Ronald Reagan, from whom I originally borrowed it.

ITEM 7: Finally, I leave the remainder of my estate to Miami Dolphins quarterback Dan Marino on the condition that he never humiliates his fans again by appearing in another movie.

JIM GOES TO THE MOVIES

Movie theaters are just lousy with remakes, from *An Affair to Remember* to *A Little Princess*.
But when Jim Carrey starts remaking movies, well, you just better watch out, because the guy's a psycho.

Good evening, ladies and gentlemen, and welcome to the Bates Motel, where even the electric sockets have no outlet.

Jim is no dummy; he's not fool enough to play the Bogart role of Sam Spade in a remake of *The Maltese Falcon*, but why not play the Sydney Greenstreet role and get a few laughs? Come on, guys, lighten up; it's only a movie, and the bird is a fake.

Didn't you always want to be one of the flying monkeys in *The Wizard of Oz*? That was Jim's great childhood wish, and in this remake he finally got the role. Showing off his versatility, he also plays Toto, too.

Jim, how could you?

In addition to playing dogs, Jim can also play cats. Besides, every actor should have the opportunity to work with **Marlon Brando**.

The deal came just weeks before Carrey's father died. Carrey was able to tell his father the good news before his death.

Six or seven years earlier, before *Ace*, before *In Living Color*, in the days when his hopes were still being recited to himself nightly while parked on Mulholland Drive, Carrey sat down one night and wrote himself a check. "For acting services rendered," it said. The figure? Ten million dollars. The date? July 4, 1995.

At his father's funeral, before the casket was closed, he tucked the check into his father's pocket.

"I wrote it as an affirmation of everything I learned," he told *Parade*. "It wasn't about money. I knew if I was making that much, I'd be working with the best people on the best material. That's always been my dream. My parents taught me to believe in miracles. My life is proof that they exist."

JIM GOES TO THE MOVIES

FILMOGRAPHY

ONCE BITTEN (1985), starring Lauren Hutton, JIM CARREY, Karen Kopins, Cleavon Little, Thomas Ballatore, Skip Lackey. Directed by Howard Storm.

PEGGY SUE GOT MARRIED (1986), starring Kathleen Turner, Nicolas Cage, Barry Miller, Catherine Hicks, Joan Allen, Kevin J. O'Connor, JIM CARREY, Lisa Jane Persky, Barbara Harris, Don Murray, Maureen O'Sullivan, Leon Ames, Helen Hunt, John Carradine, Sofia Coppola, Sachi Parker. Directed by Francis Ford Coppola.

THE DEAD POOL (1988), starring Clint Eastwood, Patricia Clarkson, Evan C. Kim, Liam Neeson, David Hunt, Michael Currie, Michael Goodwin, JAMES CARREY. Directed by Buddy Van Horn.

EARTH GIRLS ARE EASY (1989), starring Geena Davis, Jeff Goldblum, JIM CARREY, Damon Wayans, Julie Brown, Michael McKean, Charles Rocket, Larry Linville, Rick Overton, Angelyne. Directed by Julien Temple.

PINK CADILLAC (1989), starring Clint Eastwood, Bernadette Peters, Timothy Carhart, Tiffany Gail Robinson, Angela Louise Robinson, John Dennis Johnston, Geoffrey Lewis, William Hickey, JAMES CARREY. Directed by Buddy Van Horn.

HIGH STRUNG (shot in 1989, released on video in 1994). Carrey in cameo appearance.

ACE VENTURA: PET DETECTIVE (1994), starring JIM CARREY, Sean Young, Courteney Cox, Dan Marino. Directed by Tom Shadyac.

THE MASK (1994), starring JIM CARREY, Peter Riegert, Peter Greene, Amy Yasbeck, Cameron Diaz, Richard Jeni, Max (as Milo). Directed by Charles Russell.

DUMB AND DUMBER (1994), starring JIM CARREY, Jeff Daniels, Lauren Holly, Karen Duffy, Victoria Rowell, Mike Starr, Charles Rocket, Felton Perry, Harland Williams, and Teri Garr. Directed by Peter Farrelly.

BATMAN FOREVER (1995), starring Val Kilmer, Tommy Lee Jones, JIM CARREY, Nicole Kidman, Chris O'Donnell, Michael Gough, Pat Hingle. Directed by Joel Schumacher.

ACE VENTURA: WHEN NATURE CALLS (1995), starring JIM CARREY, Ian McNeice, Simon Callon. Directed by Steve Oedekerk.

MASK II (1996), starring JIM CARREY, Cameron Diaz, rest of cast and director to be announced.

CABLE GUY (1996), starring JIM CARREY, rest of cast and director to be announced.

LIAR, LIAR (1997), starring JIM CARREY, rest of cast and director to be announced.

TELEVISION

THE DUCK FACTORY (1984) lead in TV series on NBC, thirteen weeks, with Jay Tarses, Julie Payne, Teresa Ganzel, Jack Gilford, Don Messick, Clarence Gilyard Jr., Nancy Lane.

IN LIVING COLOR (1990–1993). Ensemble member of sketch comedy series on Fox TV, with Damon Wayans, Keenen Ivory Wayans, David Alan Grier, Kelly Coffield, T'Keyah "Crystal" Keymah, Kim Wayans, Tommy Davidson.

DOING TIME ON MAPLE DRIVE [TVM] (1992), Starring James B. Sikking, Bibi Besch, William McNamara, Lori Loughlin, JIM CARREY. Directed by Ken Olin.

The Jim Carrey Body Parts Jigsaw Puzzle

Get out your scissors, all you psychos, and cut out the body parts you see on this page. When put together properly, these body parts constitute one whole Jim Carrey.

Naturally, a moron could put this puzzle together, so that's why we've put you on the clock to see just how smart (or dumb) you really are. If you can assemble the jigsaw puzzle in under one minute, congratulations, you are a bona fide idiot. (After all, you did cut up this perfectly nice book, didn't you?)

If you can assemble the puzzle in under two minutes, you have the intelligence equivalent of a junior high school vice principal. If it takes you more than two minutes to put this puzzle together, a job in Washington, D.C., awaits you.

About the Authors

The Editors

SCOTT AND BARBARA SIEGEL are the authors of forty-five books, including *American Film Comedy* (Macmillan, 1994) and *The Encyclopedia of Hollywood* (Facts on File in hardcover, 1990, and Avon Books in trade paper, 1991). They have also written a considerable number of celebrity biographies, including books on Jack Nicholson, Bruce Willis, and Cybill Shepherd. The Siegels are film critics whose reviews can be heard on the Siegel Entertainment Syndicate on radio stations across the United States. In addition, Scott and Barbara write a weekly theater and cabaret column for *Drama-Logue*. The editors wish to acknowledge that they are, in fact, Jerry Lewis fans, which means they find Jim Carrey doubly hilarious.

For this volume, in addition to conceiving the project, they organized, edited, and helped design the contents, as well as wrote the introduction, and provided the photos, captions, pictorial essays and all other material not submitted by the contributors.

The Contributors

MARSHALL FINE is a film critic for the Gannett newspaper chain. He is a past president of the New York Film Critics Circle and the author of a serious book on film director Sam Peckinpah (Donald I. Fine, Inc.). Marshall wrote the Jim Carrey biography that graces this volume.

MEREDITH ANTHONY is a New York City writer who collaborated with Larry Light and Alison Power on *101 Reasons Why We're Doomed* (Avon, 1993). Writing with Alison Power, her work appears in *The Best Contemporary Women's Humor* (Crossing Press, 1994). Together with Larry Light and Alison Power, Meredith Anthony penned for this volume: Blame It on Jim, the Jim Carrey Edition of the Very Special Olympics, the Jim Carrey IQ Test, Jim's Etiquette Guide, Jim Carrey's Foul Play—A Mix 'n' Match Game, Jim Carrey's Brain, How to Talk With Your Butt, Five Things Jim Carrey Can't Do, and Jim Carrey's Dating Tips.

LARRY LIGHT has collaborated on numerous humor projects with Alison Power and Meredith Anthony. He is also, believe it or not, an editor at *Business Week*.

ALISON POWER wrote, along with Meredith Anthony, *Is Martha Stewart Living?*, a magazine parody (Southport Beach Press, 1994). She also directs public relations at New York's Central Park Zoo.

DOUGLAS BYRNE, a Jim Carrey fan since the early 1950s, who, when he isn't collecting rocks that look like toes or experimenting with meat, designs games and puzzles for kids and their parents. His kid puzzles have appeared in *Disney Adventures*, *Boys' Life*, *Sports Illustrated for Kids*, and many other children's publications. His board-game creations include Assassins/The Final Game and Mr. Meow/The First Board Game for Cats. For this volume, Douglas Byrne has prepared a puzzle, the Jim Carrey TV Network, an Interview With Sisbert and Ekel, Jim Carrey pre– and post–*Ace Ventura* endorsement lists, and four top ten lists, including Jim's Olympic Events, Favorite Foods, Favorite Jobs, and Best Pickup Lines.

HOWARD SINGER is the author of *Trivia-Mania: Movies II* (Zebra Books). He is an admissions officer at Boston College, and anybody who thinks this book is difficult reading had best make their applications directly to him. If you can write. Howard Singer took down Jim Carrey's Last Will and Testament.

PHOTOGRAPH ACKNOWLEDGMENTS

Casablanca photo courtesy of Movie Star News / *Dumb and Dumber* photo by Mark Fellman, courtesy of New Line Productions, Inc., 118

The Godfather photo courtesy of Movie Star News / *Dumb and Dumber* photo by Mark Fellman, courtesy of New Line Productions, Inc., 119

Alfred Hitchcock photo courtesy of Movie Star News/ *The Mask* photo by Darren Michaels, courtesy of New Line Productions, Inc., 115

The Maltese Falcon photo courtesy of Movie Star News / *The Mask* photo courtesy of New Line Productions, Inc., 116

The Wizard of Oz photo courtesy of Movie Star News / *Dumb and Dumber* photo by Mark Fellman, courtesy of New Line Productions, Inc., 117

Photo by Jon Farmer, courtesy of Morgan Creek Productions, Inc., 10, 58, 59, 64, 66, 125

Photo by Mark Fellman, courtesy of New Line Productions, Inc., 12, 39, 91, 94, 96, 97

Photo by Blake Little, courtesy of New Line Productions, Inc., 65

Photo by Darren Michaels, courtesy of New Line Productions, Inc., 76, 79, 81

Photo by Kimberly Wright, courtesy of New Line Productions, Inc., 37

D. C . Comics, 11, 98, 102, 103, 104, 105, 106

Globe Photos, Inc., 20, 36, 38, 48, 67, 68, 69, 70, 71, 82, 83, 84

In Living Color, 56

Morgan Creek Productions, Inc., 57, 59, 60–61, 62, 90, 112

Movie Star News, 2, 12, 13, 21, 49

New Line Productions, Inc., 8, 11, 14, 18–19, 22, 26–27, 28, 29, 30, 32, 33, 35, 41, 73, 74–75, 77, 78, 80, 85, 92, 93, 109

Photofest, 15, 42, 43, 44, 45, 46, 47, 51, 52–53, 55, 100–101, 108

Summa Video, 88

ORDER NOW! - Citadel Film & Television Books

If you like this book, you'll love Citadel Press's other television and movie books. A complete listing of these books appears below.

And if you know what books you want, why not order now? It's easy! **Just call 1-800-447-BOOK and have your MasterCard or Visa ready. (Tell the operator code #1706) Or use our toll-free sales fax 1-800-866-1966.**

FILM:
STARS
Al Pacino
Arnold Schwarzenegger
Audrey Hepburn
Barbra Streisand Films;
  Scrapbook
Bela Lugosi
Bette Davis
The Bowery Boys
Brigitte Bardot
Buster Keaton
Carole Lombard
Cary Grant
Charlie Chaplin
Clark Gable
Clint Eastwood
Curly
Dustin Hoffman
Edward G. Robinson
Elizabeth Taylor
Elvis Presley
The Elvis Scrapbook
Errol Flynn
Frank Sinatra
Gary Cooper
Gene Kelly
Gina Lollobrigida
Glenn Close
Gloria Swanson
Gregory Peck
Greta Garbo
Harrison Ford
Henry Fonda
Humphrey Bogart
Ingrid Bergman
Jack Lemmon
Jack Nicholson
James Cagney
James Dean: Behind the Scene
Jane Fonda
Jeanette MacDonald & Nelson
  Eddy
Joan Crawford
John Wayne Films; Reference
  Book; Scrapbook; Trivia Book
John Wayne's The Alamo
Judy Garland
Katharine Hepburn
Kirk Douglas
Laurel & Hardy

Lauren Bacall
Laurence Olivier
Mae West
Marilyn Monroe
Marlene Dietrich
Marlon Brando
Marx Brothers
Moe Howard & the Three
  Stooges
Olivia de Havilland
Orson Welles
Paul Newman
Peter Lorre
Rita Hayworth
Robert De Niro
Robert Redford
Sean Connery
Sexbomb: Jayne Mansfield
Shirley MacLaine
Shirley Temple
The Sinatra Scrapbook
Spencer Tracy
Steve McQueen
Three Stooges Scrapbook
Tom Hanks
Vincent Price
Warren Beatty
W.C. Fields
William Holden
William Powell
A Wonderful Life: James Stewart

DIRECTORS
Alfred Hitchcock
Cecil B. DeMille
Federico Fellini
Frank Capra
John Huston
Steven Spielberg
Woody Allen

GENRE
Black Hollywood, Vol. 1 & 2
Classic Foreign Films: From
  1960 to Today
Classic Gangster Films
Classic Science Fiction Films
Classics of the Horror Film
Cult Horror Films
Cult Science Fiction Films
Divine Images: Jesus on Screen
Early Classics of Foreign Film
Great Baseball Films

Great French Films
Great German Films
Great Italian Films
The Great War Films
Harry Warren & the Hollywood
  Musical
Hispanic Hollywood
Hollywood Bedlam: Screwball
  Comedies
The Hollywood Western
The Incredible World of 007
Jewish Image in American Film
The Lavender Screen: The Gay
  and Lesbian Films
Martial Arts Movies
Merchant Ivory Films
The Modern Horror Film
Money, Women & Guns: Crime
  Movies
More Classics of the Horror Film
Movie Psychos & Madmen
Our Huckleberry Friend: Johnny
  Mercer
Second Feature: "B" Films
They Sang! They Danced! They
  Romanced!
Thrillers
Words and Shadows: Literature
  on the Screen

DECADE
Classics of the Silent Screen
Films of the Twenties
Films of the Thirties
More Films of the '30s
Films of the Forties
Films of the Fifties
Lost Films of the '50s
Films of the Sixties
Films of the Seventies
Films of the Eighties

SPECIAL INTEREST
Bugsy (Illustrated screenplay)
The Citadel Treasury of Famous
  Movie Lines
Comic Support
The Critics Were Wrong
  (Misguided Movie Reviews)
Cutting Room Floor
Did She or Didn't She: Behind
  Bedroom Doors
Film Flubs

Film Flubs: The Sequel
Filmmaking on the Fringe
Final Curtain
First Films
Hollywood Cheesecake
Howard Hughes in Hollywood
How to Meet & Hang Out w/Stars
Jim Carrey Scrapbook
Lost Films
More Character People
Most Influential Women in Film
The Nightmare Never Ends:
  A Nightmare on Elm Street
100 Best Films of the Century
701 Toughest Movie Trivia
  Questions
Sex in Films
Sex In the Movies
Sherlock Holmes
Shot on this Site
Son of Film Flubs
Total Exposure: Nude Scenes
Who Is That?: Familiar Faces and
  Forgotten Names
Women's Book of Movie Quotes
The Worst Movies of All Time
"You Ain't Heard Nothin' Yet!"

TELEVISION:
America on the Rerun
The "Cheers" Trivia Book
Classic TV Westerns
Favorite Families of TV
Gilligan, Maynard & Me
Heather! (Locklear)
Mary, Mary, Mary! (Tyler
  Moore)
The Northern Exposure Book
The Official Andy Griffith Show
  Scrapbook
The 1001 Toughest TV Trivia
  Questions of All Time
The Quantum Leap Book
The "Seinfeld" Aptitude Test
Star Fleet Entrance Exam
The Star Trek Concordance
1201 Toughest TV Trivia
  Questions
What's Your "Frasier" IQ?
What's Your "Mad About You"
  IQ?

For a free full-color Entertainment Books brochure including the Citadel Film Series in depth and more, call 1-800-447-BOOK; or send your name and address to Citadel Film Books, Dept. 1706, 120 Enterprise Ave., Secaucus, NJ 07094.